Raising Freakishly Well-Behaved Kids
20 Principles for being the Parent your Child needs

By Jodi Ann Mullen, PhD

Foreword by Jack Canfield

*Other Books by Jodi Ann Mullen*

*Counseling Adolescents through Grief and Loss*
*Co-authored with Jody Fiorini, Research Press, 2006*

*Play Therapy Basic Training: A Guide to Learning*
*& Living the Child-Centered Play Therapy Philosophy*
*Integrative Counseling Services, 2007*

*Supervision can be Playful: Techniques for Child and Play Therapist Supervisors*
*Co-edited with Athena Drewes, Rowman & Littlefield, 2008*

*Counseling Children: A Core Issues Approach*
*Co-authored with Richard Halstead & Dale-Elizabeth Pehrsson, American Counseling Association,*
*2011*

*How Play Therapists can Engage Parents & Professionals*
*Co-authored with June Rickli, Integrative Counseling Services, 2011*

*Naughty No More: A workbook to help children make good decisions*
*Co-authored with Andrew, Leah & Michael Mullen, Balboa Press, 2013*

*Child-Centered Play Therapy Workbook: A Self-Directed Guide for Professionals.*
*Co-authored with June Rickli, Research Press, 2014*

ISBN 978-0-9796287-7-7-1

*Dedication*

*For Andrew and Leah for sharing your wisdom*
*and for Michael for being my partner in parenting and life.*

*For the children who I have had the honor of counseling;*
*you have all been teachers to me.*

*For parents who want to make childhood peaceful and full of love,*
*you have inspired me.*

## Foreword by Jack Canfield

Over the years, I have been privileged enough to meet thousands of incredible individuals and hear their stories. I have also been blessed to be able to talk with and learn from some of the most renowned individuals in their particular fields. Some of the amazing individuals I have gotten to know are children. As a parent, I have learned some very valuable lessons from children. I'm guessing, as a parent, you would like some of that wisdom and guidance as well. Who wouldn't want the best for their children? If this is you, then this book is for you.

What makes this parenting book unique is that it is from the children's perspective. For the last 25 years, Dr. Jodi Mullen has been working with children as a Mental Health Counselor and Certified Play Therapist and has taken their lessons and created a manual for parents. She has been taught many valuable lessons from the children she has had the privilege to work with. Dr. Mullen has distilled those lessons down into 20 easy to learn and easy to apply principles that have the power to transform your children's lives and your relationship with your kids. She is now sharing this wealth of knowledge with all who are willing to read it and make a few simple changes.

As adults, we tend see the world from the eyes of adults and help often comes in the form of advice or "theories" used to help other adults. These theories (that are for adults and may even work well for adults) are often inappropriately applied to children. Wouldn't it be wonderful if we took the time to listen to our children's perspective and their words to help us find ways to guide, support, and nurture them? This book does just that! The brilliance and uniqueness of this book is that it doesn't rely on advice and theories for adults, but listens to those whom we are attempting to help: our children!

Many of us are caught in our day-to-day trappings, and our "go, go, go" lives force our children to take a back seat, both literally and figuratively. We often treat children in ways that give them little to no choices and then we are confused when they make poor choices or become frightened to make any choice for themselves. To us they are acting out or misbehaving, but in reality, they are sending a message. It's time to start paying attention.

Most often children's behavior is just a reflection of the world we have created for them. Children's formative years are so critical, and it is our responsibility to be conscious of the things we say and do because we help to create their programming and belief system about themselves and their world. It is these beliefs that ultimately lead to their successes, or lack thereof. This book helps to flip that script!

We want our children to change, listen to us, and become better, yet we often aren't willing to do those things for them. Do we offer the space and patience for them to explore and be curious? Do we let our fears limit them? Do we allow them to find solutions to problems in their own way? Do we continually give them the answers and then wonder how come they have difficulty figuring things out? Do we give them encouragement to find the strength it takes to persevere in the face of adversity or difficulties? Do we complain and model how to be helpless when we are unsure and frustrated? Do we congratulate mistakes, knowing they will lead to a greater understanding or criticize and blame our children because they didn't do it "right"? This book will help you to change and improve what you do in order to help produce different results with your children. Don't we owe that to them?

Dr. Mullen and the children she has worked with offer the insights and actions necessary for the change in you that will lead to the results you are looking for with your children. Remember it starts with you, and if you are willing to read, learn, listen, grow, and work hard at this, your results will be nothing short of miraculous!

# Table of Contents

# Acknowledgements

I am surrounded with generous, supportive people. I am grateful to my friends Jill Mentes-Flack and Anabelle Gardner for reading the early drafts of this book. You helped me develop my ideas and assured me I was on the right track; I needed that. My friend support team of Judy Dunsmoor, Teresa Gentile, and Pam Caraccioli keep me laughing and loving life. Thank you, ladies for sharing the generosity of spirit, it energizes me! I also am immensely grateful to my friend, Robert Dumas who carefully and thoughtfully offered his time and talents to help me solidify ideas and connect the dots.

My colleagues and friends at Integrative Counseling Services, June Rickli and Kyle Dzintars offered advice, guidance, and an eagle-eye perspective. They are my detail people. I have a family at Integrative Counseling Services who has no shortage of energy, support, and dedication to making the world better for children and parents. You all inspire me.

The universe was looking out for me. I was lucky enough to be seated next to the author Donna Houston Murray on a flight to Philadelphia. Donna shared her time and expertise with me, 30,000 miles high, and continued to do so for more than a year after our chance meeting. Donna gave me the final push I needed to get this book to you. I am beyond grateful.

I love my parents, Gail Hernandez and Marty Weinstein. Thank you for the lessons I learned about parenting from you. I realized in my 25 years of being a child mental health professional that many children did not know that, above all else, their parents loved them. I did (and do). My siblings Rory Weinstein and Andrea Constantis are my best friends. Their support for me and what matters to me never dwindles.

Finally, my husband Michael, and my children, Leah and Andrew, have made sacrifices so I can do what I do and live my life on course. It is such a blessing that my family consists of my favorite people on the planet.

# Introduction

It's time to leave the house. I have told my daughter, who is four years old, it is time to go. I gave her an "it's almost time to go" warning five minutes ago and again one minute ago. She is ready with her shoes and jacket on and her doll in her hand. There was no fussing, no rushing, no yelling, nor stress. Ahhh, this is bliss. We are on our way to the grocery store, and she has been advised that I need her to do "Operation Cooperation" a term I stole from my sister. In the store, she is fully engaged in Operation Cooperation. I sing silly songs to her about the food that I am putting into the cart. We are in and out of the store in thirty minutes without hassles, tears, or need to bribe or bargain. We return home, unpack the groceries, and I high-five her for being so awesome. What I realize is that this little girl has taught me how to help her behave and she has taught me how to parent. She is, as my dear friend observed, "Freakishly well-behaved."

A few things that I have learned from her, and many of the children I see in my role as a mental health counselor and play therapist, are present in the above example. I know that she, like many other children, behave better when they know what to expect ("We are going to the store today. We are leaving in five minutes."), and what your expectations for them are (Operation Cooperation). I have learned that children like structure and stability. When you tell them what to expect and what your expectations are you provide them with these. Children have also taught me that they like us parents to notice when they are good and are behaving good. They have taught me that that should be acknowledged (the high-five).

Early on in my role as a parent, I realized I benefited greatly from my education and professional preparation as a counselor and play therapist. I looked around at all the well-meaning, good-intentioned, smart, loving, and thoughtful parents making mistakes they swore as children they would never make when they became parents, like saying," "Because I said so," or making their child eat their vegetables. The truth is we all make mistakes as parents (I make them daily). I believe though, that if we had a guide we could follow, we could do better and all raise freakishly well-behaved children who feel as good about themselves as their behavior would indicate.

Guilt. Shame. Confusion. Fear. Most of my meetings with parents start off this way. Parents bring their children to a mental health counselor typically feeling like failures. They are sure, and state, "We screwed up our kid." They have many questions: "Why won't my child listen to me? Do you think I should have taken his favorite toy away? Do you think she is mentally ill? Do you think something bad happened to her?" Ultimately, parents want to know why their children are behaving, actually misbehaving, in particular ways. They have exhausted all of their ideas. They worry their children are beyond repair. Their children are not, and neither are they.

The secret is this: much of our fear, frustration, embarrassment, and guilt about our children, their behavior, and our parenting can be eliminated: when we listen to our children. In this book, the ideas about parenting come from children. Who is a better authority on what works (and what doesn't) in parenting than children?

*As to methods there may be a million and then some, but principles are few.*
*The man who grasps principles can successfully select his own methods.*
*The man who tries methods, ignoring principles, is sure to have trouble.*
*Ralph Waldo Emerson*

What makes this parenting book different is that the focus is on the underlying principles of effective parenting. This is not so much a "How-to" parenting technique book (although I will offer some examples of techniques) as it is a parenting principle and values book. What I mean by that is that effective parenting comes from what you do and through understanding why you do it. The why is what makes us good parents the techniques and behaviors can differ parent to parent or even with the different children in your family, but the principles stay the same.

I learned these principles from some very wise teachers: children. I have the honor of having close relationships with children. I get to spend one-on-one time with them. If I have done my job well, they feel safe and comfortable around me. Because of that, because they are not afraid I will judge them or that they will "get in trouble" with me, I get a view of childhood without much censoring.

It is in this safe, comfortable, and therapeutic environment that I have been able to learn from children what they need from their parents. This book is a collection of those lessons. What you will find in this book are 20 principles for effective parenting from the perspectives of children. Many of the principles are intuitive and seem simple, but be prepared because putting them into to practice takes time and patience (especially with yourself). Some of the principles may seem to defy what you have learned in the past about parenting. This is good news. Most of what we know about parenting comes from other adults. These lessons on parenting come from children.

Often as parents we want to know why a child is behaving a certain way. Let's be honest: we want to know why she is misbehaving. Although we can guess and hypothesize, only the child herself really knows. Sometimes she can express the reason for misbehaving verbally like, "I hate eating peas, that's why I threw them across the table." But most of the time children have not reached the necessary verbal and conceptual development milestones to clear up the why of the misbehavior for us.

Even if they cannot articulate it, they do know why. This is why it is so crucial to learn about what works in parenting from the perspectives of children while they are still children, before those lessons are distorted through the lens of development to adulthood. Because the principles come from the perspectives of children, they have an inherent simplicity that is focused on the parent-child relationship. Following these child-centered principles fosters parent-child relationships based in love and respect. When a loving and respectful parent-child relationship is the foundation for parenting and discipline, the result is well-behaved, thoughtful, and social-conscious children.

*Even when freshly washed and relieved of all obvious confections,*
*children tend to be sticky.*
*Fran Lebowitz, author*

# Principle #1

## I love you no matter what. Love me that way too

.

*Accept the children the way we accept trees—with gratitude, because they are a blessing—but do not have expectations or desires. You don't expect trees to change, you love them as they are. Isabel Allende, author*

Lauren is a beautiful little girl. She is quiet. She loves to play outside. She is also miserable. She suffers with nightmares, feeling sad most of the day, everyday, and frequently fights with her sister. She also has stolen items from her classmates and lies about many things. Her parents brought her to me for counseling because her grades in school are "terrible." I asked her parents to define terrible; she has a low "B" average.

Lauren's parents are both formally educated. How both their children perform in school is of the highest importance to them. According to her parents, Lauren is bright, but she doesn't apply herself. She frequently forgets her homework or does it without much care. Many of us, whether we have a formal education or not, value education and can easily relate to Lauren's parents' concerns and frustrations.

As it turns out, thanks to comprehensive testing done by the school psychologist, we were able to get some reliable information about Lauren. Lauren actually didn't perform as well as might have been expected on several different measures of her intelligence. The school psychologist concluded, "Lauren is a great kid with perfectly average, at best, intelligence."

Somehow in all the arguments, pleadings, negotiations and bribes about her school performance, Lauren got the idea that her parents didn't value her if she did not earn A's like her older sister. How do I know this? Lauren said randomly (kids do that a lot) during her counseling session, "My parents don't love me." I asked her how she knew this. Her reply, "They only love me if I get A's, I get B's."

Now, did Lauren's parents love her? Of course, they did! What they did not do was demonstrate that. Although their preference was for her to earn A's in school, it was not a deal breaker for their love when she earned less than an A.

In the 25 years, I have been a helping professional, I have worked with children who have suffered many injustices and traumas at the hands of their parents. I am talking about severe neglect, physical, and sexual abuse. Do you know what the common theme is among these children? They all still love and want to be loved by their parents. One eight-year-old boy I worked with, who was literally in a body cast from physical abuse from the assault by his mother, said in a counseling session, "I still love my mom, I wished she would still love me."

What can we learn from children about how to be good parents? It's fairly simple: we must love our children unconditionally. It is not enough to feel that or say it we must behave accordingly. That was what went wrong with Lauren's parenting: her parents felt it and said it, but they did not act like they loved her unconditionally, at least from Lauren's perspective, and that is what matters.

*What it's like to be a parent: It's one of the hardest things you'll ever do but in exchange it teaches you the meaning of unconditional love.*
*Nicholas Sparks, novelist & screenwriter, The Wedding*

What does unconditional love mean anyway? What it means for us, as parents, is that we love our children regardless of their behavior, their choice of friends, their lack of athleticism, and their disgraceful taste in music. Like most of the 20 parenting principles, this sounds simple, it is not.

The way to love your children unconditionally is grounded in accepting and respecting. By that I mean you have to practice (I mean it, it takes practice) accepting your child as she is and respecting the person she is. Put it this way: you don't have to accept unacceptable behavior like stealing or lying, but you do have to find a way to show your child that although you do not find their behavior or choice acceptable, you love them.

 When your little one writes on the window with permanent marker, you can do what I did which was combination of yelling and crying followed by telling my child to get away from me (an example of what not to do). You can stop in your tracks, leave the immediate area (yell and cry on the inside) and then return to your child and the scene. In my fantasy this is how I would have handled it: Upon returning to the scene, I would have said to my child, "That this is not acceptable and I am upset. You cannot use markers on the window, but you can use them on paper or in a coloring book. You have to help me clean the window. If you use markers anywhere but on paper or the coloring book again, I will take your markers away. I love you even though I am mad about the window."

I know. I know. That's the ideal and it would be super difficult to carry out. It is possible. When you practice, it becomes routine. The result: your child feels loved unconditionally and that's the most awesome feeling. You know that feeling because that's the way your child loves you.

*When you look into your mother's eyes, you know*
*that is the purest love you can find on this earth.*
*Mitch Albom, author, For One More Day*

Principle #2

Treat me with respect.

*Careful the things you say, children will listen.*
*Careful the things you do, children will see and learn.*
*Stephen Sondheim, in Into the Woods*

Yesterday when I was having my eye exam, my eye doctor, who is also my son's eye doctor and former soccer coach said, "I have to tell you, your son is the best-behaved child I have ever met." I of course, felt very proud of him and felt like my husband and I can take some credit for that. What occurred to me though is how this man interacted with my son as his coach and subsequently as his eye doctor. In every exchange, he was respectful to my son.

Respect has an element of reciprocity that children are hardly afforded. Children are told to respect their elders as if all elders deserve their respect. It is typically a blanket statement or even a rule that children have to follow. They have to be respectful to all adults, in all settings, in all situations. This is a poor parenting policy for a number of reasons. I will share the most grave and serious reason.

I'm going to be blunt: Children who believe they must respect adults under all circumstances are often the same children who I work with in counseling who have been victimized. They won't tell a safe adult what a perpetrating adult did to them for many reasons. I have clients ranging from age four to 74 tell me the reason they never told anyone about the abuse was because they were told they had to listen to adults and do what adults say. The default is that adults always know better than children and are always right. It's dangerous for your children to believe this.

Are children expected to be respectful to adults who are disrespectful to them? As an adult, are you respectful to people who are disrespectful to you? During counseling sessions, I have had many children and adolescents talk about the way they are treated by teachers and other school officials. Some recognized the double standard and will say, "Why do I have to be respectful to Mr. Hernandez? He makes fun of me." There's really only one authentic answer here and that is: "Because you have to be respectful to him. He's your teacher." How does a child make sense of that? You are essentially asking your children to be passive, to let others treat them disrespectfully, and to not stand up for what is important to them. Those are not the lessons well-adjusted, pro-social, good citizens have under the surface. On the contrary, they are assertive, courageous, and hold themselves in high regard.

Children do not typically need to be taught to be respectful of adults who are respectful to them. However, in the instances that your child is being disrespectful to an adult who is respectful, you will need to concretely point this out to your child. It is best if you keep what you say concrete and brief like, "Mr. Dzintars has always been respectful to you. You are not being respectful to him." I typically do this in private if I can, and I am specific about how my child is being disrespectful saying something like, "I know you think you are being funny when you make fun of Mr. Dzintars' hat. It's not funny. It's disrespectful."

Children, however, do need some guidance in how to handle adults who are disrespectful to them. It is very difficult for them as children to stand up for themselves with adults or to point out the hypocrisy of an adult who demands respect, but does not give it. There are a couple of different strategies you can use here.

Many times, I choose to step in and model clear and assertive communication for my children. I might say something like, "I think Andrew (my son) is having a hard time being respectful to you because he does not feel respected when he's being yelled at in front of his team." In this example, I would say it in front of my son, to the coach privately. Another option is to quietly and privately say to your child, "I can see Mrs. Lawton is being disrespectful to you. I would be proud of you if you didn't talk back and sass her. I would also be proud of you if you told her you don't like being called 'Andy.' I know you have already told her this many times before."

It's important to have a follow-up conversation with your child about disrespectful people and how to respond to them, especially when the disrespectful person is an adult. Disrespect does not need to be met with disrespect. I teach and help my children as well as my clients to be authentic. Tell the disrespectful person what your experience is (this works with adults too). Try this sentence starter: "I feel disrespected when…" Practice this with your children and encourage them to use it even with you. You can model this assertiveness by using this same model in your life and even with them.

*What a child doesn't receive he can seldom later give.*
*P.D. James, Time to Be in Earnest*

**A Mother F'er**
"Hey Jodi guess what happened to me at school today?" Annabelle asked. I replied, "You know I hate guessing games. Um, let's see. Ok, you got an 'A' on your science mid-term?" Annabelle appreciates the humor in this and said, "Nope, got expelled for calling my math teacher a Mother F'er, which she is!"

Annabelle is a problem. At fourteen-years-old she is in her fourth foster care home in six months. No one wants to deal with her sneaking out, bad attitude, drug use, indiscriminate sexual behavior, and vulgar language. She behaves this way at home and at school, where she has been suspended for a host of disrespectful behavior six times over the past two years.

Annabelle has problems. She had been severely abused and neglected for most of her life. Her parents are chemically addicted, her father incarcerated. Neither of her parents kept her safe. She has a documented learning disability and suffers from severe anxiety related to the traumas she has endured.

I was feeling confused by Annabelle's story. An eighth grader could really get expelled for saying "Mother F'er." That seemed a little harsh to me. I asked, "You got expelled for calling her a Mother F'er. I mean F'er, that doesn't seem like expulsion material." Annabelle laughed, "You're funny. I didn't say F'er to her, I used that whole word!"

Now that was interesting to me. In my counseling office children, adolescents and adults alike are not restricted in the language they use to tell their stories and share their experiences. Colorful and powerful language is understood from precisely that perspective. If Annabelle wanted to use the full term for F'er in my office during our session, I would not have even batted an eye-lash, but she didn't; I wondered out loud why by saying, "I'm curious about you not choosing to say the "F" word here, in front of me." Annabelle answered, as if were the simplest question she could have been asked, "Because you respect me, so I respect you."

*Respect for right conduct is felt by everybody.*
*Jane Austen, Novelist*

Somehow along the way from childhood to adulthood, we have forgotten what it is like to be respected as a child. We have also forgotten what it is like to be disrespected. I know that many of us have disconnected with these memories because if we held onto them we surely would not act disrespectfully to children, particularly our own.

I am going to ask you to access some of those memories. Let's take the negative experiences first. Please list three experiences you had as a child where you felt like you were disrespected by an adult. Examples may include being accused of something you did not do, lying, being talked down to, and being talked about as if you were not there.

| |
|---|
| 1. |
| 2. |
| 3. |

Now, access those special memories of feeling respected by an adult. Jot down three of those memories.

| |
|---|
| 1. |
| 2. |
| 3. |

One last thing, now write down three lessons you can take away from the examples you provided directly above to take immediate action to be more respectful to your child.

| |
|---|
| 1. |
| 2. |
| 3. |

GOOD FOR YOU!!! Now post these up somewhere to remind yourself. I bet you feel better already about your relationship with your child. You think you feel good now, wait until you see the results when you consistently practice this with you child!

*The bond that links your true family is not one of blood,*
*but of respect and joy in each other's life.*
*Richard David Bach, Writer*

## Principle #3

### Catch me behaving.

*If your baby is beautiful and perfect, never cries or fusses, sleeps on schedule and burps on demand, an angel all the time, you're the grandma.*
*Theresa Bloomingdale*

My guess is if you are reading this book you realized that sometimes you are not sure what to do as a parent. You have realized you are not perfect and neither are your children (behaviorally speaking, of course). When your child misbehaves, this discomfort seems to grow so that we become even more self-conscious about our parenting.

Many of the parents, who I work with professionally, as well as those who are my friends and family members, will ask about their parenting, "What am I doing wrong?" No one has ever asked, "What am I doing right?" I decided to ask you that question (I have a good reason for it, you'll see). Also, even by this point in the book, I bet you have said to yourself, "Ha. Yes! I already do that! Hooray for me!" and have felt a sense of validation and pride about your parenting. I just know that you have been doing some things well all along and that you are feeling delighted about them. Take a few minutes to write down some of the things you are most proud of in your role as a parent. I have given you space for 10 statements. Feel free to write as many as possible. If you have more than ten, keep going. Write until you have exhausted the list, then come back to it and add more.

1. _____

2. _____

3. _____

4. _____

5. _____

6. _____

7. _____

8. _____

9. _____

10. _____

The reason I asked you to do this is because in order to catch your child behaving well, you need to be able to do that for yourself first. If you can catch yourself being a good parent, then surely you can catch your child behaving.

**Gary is a monster**

I was actually a little scared to work with Gary because of the way his mother described him when she called to request counseling services for her son. She described him as violent and cunning. She said of her son, "He's evil. He's mean. We want him out of our house."

I geared up for my first session with Gary. I was prepared to have to set many limits, and that my personal safety was likely to be in jeopardy. I looked him over quickly as he and his Mom entered the waiting area. He didn't look any more evil than any other six-year-old boy I had worked with. Once we got in to the therapeutic playroom I was sure he would reveal his terrible self.

He didn't. He never did. He revealed what it was like to be rejected by your parents and older siblings. In a role play he created in his Play Therapy session, Gary as the Mom said to me as the child, "I don't love you, get over it." I pretended to cry. Still in role he said, "I wish you were never born. I hate you even more when you cry."

I set up a time to meet with Gary's parents. I let them know that I thought Gary had a terrific prognosis. He demonstrated good manners, empathy and listening skills in his sessions. His parents dismissed my observations. Instead they told me everything Gary had done wrong in the past two weeks. He had hit his sister, spilled his drink on the floor, and made a mess in the bathroom with toothpaste. I explained that although those examples surely are annoying to us as parents, they don't make Gary awful. His mother replied, "He's a monster."

A monster? Gary? I needed his parents to find the good in Gary. I asked them to look for it, even little things. I suggested we meet again the next week and that they should come prepared by sharing three examples of catching Gary behaving in prosocial ways. In fact, I told them, "I will only meet with you after you have found three things. See if you can catch him saying please or thank you. Maybe you can notice him being kind to his sisters?" How did his parents respond? Here's what his Dad said, "We didn't bring him here for that. Just fix him." My heart broke.

As parents, we can be detectives. We are working on the most important case of our career, and lives depend on it. We have to find our children doing good things and being kind and thoughtful people. We have to notice and tell them we notice when they hold the door open for Grandma, when they share a smile, when they help set the table or brush their teeth after we only asked once.
Just today I caught my children doing the following things. They:

- Cleaned up without being asked.
- Helped me clear off the dinner table.
- Got right into the shower when prompted.
- Were kind to each other.
- Created a hilarious video on the iPad, together!
- Cleaned up the craft area without being asked.

- Gave me hugs.
- Paid attention to and played with the cats.
- Helped make dinner.
- Stuck with a task even though frustrated.
- Were silly and got me to be silly.

In the past 24 hours what has your child been up to? What has he or she done that can be viewed as good behavior, or a way of being that you are proud of? I bet you can come up with at least five items for your list (make that five per child, so if you have two kids, there should be five for each of them, for total of ten).

1. _____

2. _____

3. _____

4. _____

5. _____

My guess is that you did not overtly acknowledge what you noticed to your child when you noticed it. That's your homework. Tomorrow, when you catch her doing something, behaving in a way that you are proud of, doing something you hope she does again, tell her. For example, I could have said to my children today, "I love when you guys work together so cooperatively," or "Thank you two for being silly and getting me to be silly also." Here's one more example based on my list: "I am thrilled that you guys cleaned up the craft area. Now I don't have to do it and I can use that time to hang out with you."

*We worry about what a child will be tomorrow, yet we forget that he is someone today.*
*Stacia Tauscher*

I think we all have experiences at home or at the work place where we are proud of something we have done. We feel good about organizing the lids to the plastic containers, bringing bagels to the office just because, or making a delicious dinner. What's that like for you when those acts go unacknowledged (I am not suggesting you did any of that to be acknowledged)? What about when someone does notice and shares appreciation of you with you? What's that like? Use the table below to compare the impact of those experiences.

| Feelings when Unacknowledged | Feelings when Appreciated |
|---|---|
|  |  |
|  |  |
|  |  |
|  |  |
|  |  |

Keep those feelings in mind, how nice it feels to be appreciated and acknowledged, and how disappointing it is when you make an effort to do something, or what you feel is right and do not get noticed. Now imagine that experience is intertwined with the person who means the most to you (in this example your parent or parents). Add in what it would be like if you cannot make sense of the lack of attention or appreciation (developmentally many children are just not there yet with the way their thinking works). What I want to get at is it will feel good to you and your child when you notice what he is doing well, and when he is behaving. As humans, we all love attention and recognition so not only will it feel good, it will encourage more of that behavior and way of being. It's a big win for parents and kids alike!

*We cannot always build the future of our youth, but we can build our youth for the future.*
*Franklin Delano Roosevelt*

Principle #4

Let me experience power and control by giving me choices
(but don't overwhelm me).

*The strongest principle of growth lies in the human choice.*
*George Eliot, novelist*

I know it sometimes feels like your child has a lot of power and control. I have even heard parents say about their child "He runs the house and he's only four!" The issue of power and control in the parent-child relationship is complex. If you give children too much power and/or control they become difficult to parent, and if you don't give them enough, well, they become difficult to parent. Where well-intentioned parents typically go wrong is by offering too much power and control. Parents give too many choices, thereby overwhelming the child. Sometimes parents do not allow choices when they can, thereby not permitting their child to experience being in charge or making decisions.

As a parent, you have to strike the right balance. The tricky part, and this is tricky with regard to this principle as well as the other nineteen, is the balance being different for each child and family, and may need to be adjusted as children grow and family dynamics change. For instance, the power balance will look different when you are parenting a four-year-old versus a ten-year-old. The power difference will need shifting when that same four-year-old begins attending school. The power balance will likely need adjusting when a new baby comes into the family. In essence, the principle stays the same; it's the way you employ the principle that changes as your family changes and your child grows up. You will notice that parenting techniques like "time-outs" work well when your child is three but are not nearly as effective when your child is eleven. Therefore, I encourage you to focus on the principle rather than the technique. If you stick to the principle, you will find or develop your own techniques that adapt to your ever-changing child.

Now that you have a sense of the dynamic role of power and control, I want to share something that I have learned from children. I have learned that if you view the world from their perspective (that's empathy, and I'll talk more about it in Principle 19), children truly lack power and control. Children do not feel powerful; they feel powerless. By giving children the opportunity for power or control or even the illusion of it, you empower them and allow them to experience the responsibility that comes with power or control. The responsibility that comes with having some power and control will have a life-long impact. Your child will learn how to make decisions, problem solve, and deal with the natural consequences that emerge from the decisions they make. Doesn't that sound like a terrific thing? I know you want that for your child. Imagine this, by employing this principle consistently, your child will learn how to take responsibility for her behavior and actions; something we adults often struggle with ourselves and observe our teenagers struggling with too.

One way you can give your child a sense of power and control is by giving your child an opportunity to make a choice, but too many choices can be overwhelming and anxiety provoking. You would not want to ask, "What do you want for lunch, peanut butter and jelly, grilled cheese, a ham sandwich, ravioli, or cereal?" There are too many choices. Worse yet would be leaving it open-ended like, "What do you want for lunch, I'll make whatever you like." Both examples sound nice, even nurturing. However, there is too much choice and that can be stressful for children.

What you want to do is set it up so you are giving a choice between one thing and another. Giving your child a choice between two things gives your child a sense of power and an opportunity to advocate and assert himself without feeling overwhelmed and potentially anxious. What you don't want to do is list all the possibilities for lunch; instead you can ask, "Would you rather have a grilled cheese or peanut butter and jelly sandwich?" What happens if the child responds with "I want tuna fish." Tuna fish wasn't a choice, so you remind the child of the choices by asking again. You may be thinking, "Seriously it's not a big deal to open a can of tuna, can't I just do that?" You can if you are comfortable demonstrating to your child that you are not a person of your word (see Principle 15). You gave two choices; the child needs to pick one.

*As a child, my family's menu consisted of two choices: take it, or leave it.*
*Buddy Hackett, comedian*

Children (like adults) like to test the limits of people; they are assessing possibilities. Asking for tuna when it was not a choice is a test, a clever test, of both people and possibilities. By this I mean, the child is testing you to see if you will stick to your word or if you can be nudged. This assessment of you will be important for future interactions with you. If you chose to make the tuna, will you give in when they ask for an extra thirty minutes to stay up past bedtime, or will you buy that toy even though you said "No?" See how this becomes a problem? No tuna; either grilled cheese or peanut butter and jelly.

*A comment about food choices: Often power struggles around food have to do with wanting our children to make healthy food choices. The best way to get that to happen is by modeling healthy food choices; they're watching you! Also, I want you to think about this: as adults, we do not eat food we find disgusting just because it is good for us. We have to like the flavor and the consistency or we are going to pass on that kale no matter how nutritionally magical it is. Be considerate of your child's opinion when deciding if the struggle is worth it with regard to food choice.*

A good tip when dealing with these slick negotiators, also referred to as kids, is to communicate directly and concretely with children. When you are offering a choice, be clear that they have the luxury of choice. Instead of saying "Which towel for after your bath, blue or purple?" illuminate that she is being given an opportunity for choice by using the word "choice" in your offer, "It's your choice, the blue towel or the purple one."

Sometimes there are not choices. There are times when we as adults do not have choices either, so this principle is well grounded in reality. For example, bedtime is not a choice, whether your child goes to school is not a choice, dress that is appropriate for climate and age is not a choice. Children know how to wear you down so they get their way. No choice, means no negotiation. You must not flounder here (more about this in Principle 15).

## Let me tell you about Arline

I am particularly fond of the feisty kids. Arline is a feisty kid. At age six, and in first grade, she is full of energy. She is also an expert tester. She has a strong personality, is passionate and powerful. She is not an easy child to parent; she is strong-willed (strong-willed daughters are difficult to raise, but I wouldn't have it any other way, would you?). Her parents consulted me in my role as a mental health counselor because Arline is "running the show at home."

Her loving and doting parents want to make sure she is safe, has her needs met, and experiences some of the luxuries they can afford to provide for her. Arline frequently tells them she hates them; she has scribbled swear words on notes and left them for her parents. She says she wants to run away, and she throws tantrums. She also is very affectionate, smart, and a cunning negotiator. When does affectionate and clever Arline turn into Arline the terrible? Her parents answer in unison and without a second of thought, "When she doesn't get her way." The thing is she only doesn't get her way briefly because her parents admit they cave in. Her father said, "I just want to give my little girl everything she wants." OH NO.

Now look, it is ok to want to give your child everything she or he wants, but it's not okay to actually do that; that's not the way the world works and I'm not sure it's even possible.

Back to Arline. I was able to watch some parent-child interactions when Arline came home from school. Arline was spunky and cheerful upon arriving home. She said to her mother, "Get me cookies. I'll be watching my show." Her mother said that she first had to do her homework. Arline was not having it. "I said I was having cookies then watching my show." Ah ha! That side of Arline now shows up. Arline's mother tells her no in several different ways and then enters into negotiations with Arline. Poor Mom doesn't stand a chance. Arline is offered cookies first, then homework, then her show. Arline states clearly, "That's not going to happen." Her mother is naturally ticked by this, and a power struggle emerges. Arline's mom begins to log a series of examples of Arline's disrespectfulness, and Arline turns on the TV and watches her show, smirking. Arline's mom points out to me this is what makes her crazy.

Of course, Arline's mom is feeling crazy; she gave away her power (Arline knew she would). Let me break this game down like sport analysts break down plays in football games. The power dynamic is obvious in the first interaction between Mom and Arline when Arline orders her to get cookies and tells her what she will be doing. That's too much power for Arline. She doesn't get anxious or overwhelmed by this power. Instead she wields it like a sword. She cuts down her mother's sense of power, her control, and her parenting-esteem. Mom had several opportunities to clearly state to Arline what her choices were and were not. She could indeed have cookies (if she asked respectfully) and watch her show, if she chose to do her homework first. Mom would have to repeat this and stick to it. Arline can't manage the amount of power and control she has. Her mom (and dad) have to take back some of it by limiting her choices.

> *The thing that impresses me most about America*
> *is the way parents obey their children.*
> *Edward, Duke of Windsor*

Power and choice can circumvent power struggles between you and your child. The bedtime struggle becomes, "you can choose to go to bed now, at your bedtime, or in five minutes. If you choose five minutes from now, you choose no bedtime cuddle." The going to school struggle becomes, "you can choose to get your lunch ready for school now or you will have to buy lunch; either way the bus will be here in fifteen minutes." The dress struggle becomes, "you cannot wear those shorts because it is snowing outside, but you can choose between jeans or sweat pants."

## Shane is wearing sneakers two sizes too big

Shane's mom called me at home at seven in the morning. I was surprised to have this counseling client's mom call me at home and before eight a.m.! I figured something must be very wrong. I could hear Shane screaming in the background—yes, something was very wrong.

I had been seeing Shane for counseling for a few months. His school counselor referred him for services because he was a target of frequent bullying. Shane lacked self-confidence and was very passive.

What I did not know about Shane was that he had two pairs of sneakers. The pair he typically wore and a pair in his closet that his mom got on sale that were put aside for when he grew into them. The thing was that the pair that Mom put aside were so much cooler than the pair that currently fit Shane. What was all that screaming about?

Shane was screaming, throwing things, punching himself and threatening to run away because he wanted to wear the cooler, although ill-fitting, sneakers. He was certainly overreacting. However, because Shane had such limited opportunities for choice both at home and at school, this sneaker thing came to represent his desperation for some sense of power.

I suggested to his mother that she give him a choice, "Tell Shane he can choose to wear the sneakers that are too big on him. If they are uncomfortable or make it difficult for him to walk properly that is directly because of the choice he made to wear them." About twenty-five seconds of quiet followed. Shane's mom then said, "I do have to give him control over some things I guess." She relayed the choice message to Shane who responded, "Thanks, Mom, I like picking out my own clothes."

Sometimes it is that simple, although most of the time it is not. Shane's mom needed parent coaching in that moment. She became more invested in her son's counseling and capitalized on additional parent coaching. She practiced and made changes. It was not at all simple or easy. It was, however, the key to Shane's improved mental health and a solid relationship between Mom and Shane.

*We need to teach the next generation of children from day one that they are responsible for their lives. Mankind's greatest gift, also its greatest curse, is that we have free choice. We can make our choices built from love or from fear.*
*Elisabeth Kubler-Ross, psychiatrist*

Principle #5

Listen to me

*Most of the successful people I've known are the ones who do*
*more listening than talking.*
*Bernard Baruch, financier & political consultant*

As a trained mental health counselor, I know the most important thing you can do for some-one is to listen to them. My clients—young children, teenagers, and adults, routinely express that they love coming to counseling because they know I am listening. One of my forty-year-old clients said, "I love that you listen to me so much; it doesn't even matter that I have to pay you to do it!"

Listening to children is different than listening to adults though. Listening, I mean true, hard-core, "I am totally attentive" listening is a difficult enough task between adults, but it is more complicated when the communication is adult-child.

Think of children as if they are from another planet. On the planet "Childhood" they commu-nicate differently than on our planet, "Adulthood." On Childhood, communication is largely non-verbal and through play. Where adults talk things out, children act them out. Therefore, in order to truly listen to children, you have to listen to their non-verbal communication, and to their play.

Your ability to listen to your child will directly affect your ability to communicate with them. Bet-ter communication means a better relationship.
In order to listen to the non-verbal expression of children, you have to engage your observa-tion skills. Watch facial expressions closely; is that an angry expression or is that frustration or maybe even fear? As the parent, you are the best person to decipher the facial expression of your child.

If you want to demonstrate to your child (it doesn't matter how old OR young), share with your child what you see. It is how you respond to them that will show you are listening. For example, you can say, "You look mad." If you are correct, your child will feel listened to and understood. If you are wrong and your child was not mad but annoyed there are benefits to your relationship with your child too!

If you made an effort to understand your child's feeling, and got it wrong, your child now knows: 1) my parent is trying to listen (and that earns you points in the form of credibility when you are off target and wrong) and 2) your child might correct you, and tell you what is right. You gain credits with your child because you are making an effort, and 3) You stand a better chance of correctly understanding their non-verbal communication next time around. Sometimes your child will even correct you, and that is a gift. This is where you reread the words and think "Gift? What?" Hold on, stay with me. Here's what you can take away from that interaction where you were wrong and then corrected by your child:

1) Your child feels safe enough to correct you, meaning your child is not afraid of you. If your little guy feels safe enough to tell you when you are wrong, he will feel safe to tell you other things as well.

2) Your child can identify his own state of feeling and knows what he is NOT feeling.

3) Your child knows how to verbally express her feelings. If your child can verbally express her feelings, she does not have to act them out. There is a real benefit in that especially when the feeling is anger.

4) Your child has the esteem to tell or show you what his internal experience is like.

Everything on the above list can come from you being wrong (and willing to hear that feedback), and that is AWESOME. These exchanges with your child are authentic and based in honesty and trust, the foundation of all good relationships.

Another way to be sure you are listening to your child is to play with them. When children play, they show you how they see their world.

**Our little Leah is cute, but strange.**

When our daughter, Leah, our first born, was two years old, I observed her playing in our family room. She had collected almost twenty dish towels and washcloths and laid them out side by side on the floor. On each towel or cloth, she put a baby doll or stuffed animal. She then walked between the towels, one on her right and one on her left, and moved her hands over each doll on the towel in a circular pattern. She did this repeatedly over each and every doll. I watched her closely during this play and even fetched my husband from what he was busy doing to point out this interesting play to him. I said to him, (now remember I am a mental health counselor and play therapist), "She's really odd." We had a good laugh, but it was really strange.

Fast forward to later that week. I had to pick Leah up from her daycare early because she had a doctor's appointment. I arrived during naptime and walked into this scene: a room full of twenty children, sleeping on cots on the floor. The daycare providers sat between the children and rubbed their backs in a circular fashion. Ah-ha!

Leah playing that way wasn't strange; it was her playing out her life. Her play was communicating her experience. All children do that, yours included. If you watch, or better yet, join them in play, you are actually listening to them.

Here are some additional fundamentals for listening to children.

Listen without distractions. For example, let the phone ring, stop washing the dishes, and step away from the computer. Because children communicate so well non-verbally, they need to be able to read your communications as well. Get down on the child's level physically. This means you may have to crouch down to listen to your child. From this vantage point you have the best chance at reading facial expressions accurately and vice versa. This helps you listen to your child and also helps your child listen to you.

Drs. Garry Landreth and Sue Bratton (2006), world-renowned play therapists, suggest this technique for listening to your child even when they want your attention at an inopportune time, like when you are on the phone:

Say to the person on the phone, "Can you hold on for thirty seconds? I'm coming right back." Then bend down and get at eye level with your child. For the next thirty seconds give your child your undivided attention. You want to listen as if what he is saying or showing you is the most important communication on the planet. When the thirty seconds is up, state clearly to your child that you are going to return to your conversation on the phone. This burst of attention and attentive listening often works with children because you are demonstrating to your child through listening, even in bursts, that she is important.

*The greatest deficit in America isn't the trade deficit.*
*It's the attention deficit of our children.*
*The average child gets fourteen minutes of attention a day from each of his parents.*
*So the greatest thing you can give a kid is time spent listening to him or her.*
*Jack Canfield, motivational speaker & author*

Principle # 6

If you tell me what I can't do
please also tell me what I can do.

*Call them rules or call them limits, good ones, I believe, have this in common:*
*They serve reasonable purposes; they are practical and within a child's capability; they are consis-*
*tent; and they are an expression of loving concern.*
*Fred Rogers, educator & television host*

Children experience a great deal of don'ts.
"Don't talk to me that way."
"Don't pick your nose."
"Don't say those words."
"Don't eat that with your fingers."

Limits are a crucial component of good parenting. Children need us to tell them "Don't" "No" until they can make those decisions responsibly on their own (for more about saying NO see Principle 17). It helps make them feel safe, cared for, loved, and contained. Limits also help children learn values, social expectancies, and manners.

Children translate limits to have alternative meanings. Let's take another look at the list above and look at what children my make of those limits.

"Don't talk to me that way" becomes "Your view does not matter."
"Don't pick your nose" becomes "You're disgusting."
"Don't say those words" becomes "You're naughty."
"Don't eat that with your fingers" becomes "I'm embarrassed by you."

In order to best protect our children from hearing negative messages that they will internalize and hold onto as adults, we need to do a few things to polish up those important limits. When we set limits on behavior, we should be overt and clear about why we are setting the limit. Again, let's return to our example list and see what that looks like.

"Don't talk to me that way, it is disrespectful. I am respectful to you."
"Don't pick your nose, it is yucky."
"Don't say those words. I don't like hearing them, or you saying them."
"Don't eat that with your fingers. I like you to use your good manners."

Those might not seem like the best reasons to set limits for a child. Many of the limits we set for children are unnecessary. It is good to practice to recognize why you are setting a limit before you do. Limits should always be set when safety is the issue. Behaviors where the child might hurt herself, someone else, or destroy property are all valid reasons for setting limits. Let's look at the steps of limiting setting.

First you have to decide to set the limit. How you decide to set limits is mostly personal. I would suggest that you always set limits around safety. I do not let my children hurt themselves, anyone else, or destroy property. Children are concrete thinkers. This means when I tell my young child, "We will leave in five seconds," that if she counts to five it will be time to go. Recognizing that children are concrete thinkers is especially important in limit setting. If you tell your child it is not ok to smack her sister, that means it's not ok for you to smack her sister either.

**Noah's Lesson**
Noah was referred to play therapy because he would not speak in school. By the time he reached second grade this was viewed as a severe situation. Like many of the children that I have worked with who won't speak in school, Noah did not display the same problem in play therapy sessions. In fact, Noah was extremely talkative through our session, barely stopping long enough to take a breath!

Noah taught me valuable lessons about parenting, spanking, and concrete thinking all in one exchange. Upon entering the play therapy room Noah asked, "Jodi, how come I got in trouble for hitting my baby brother?" I responded, "You are confused why you would get in trouble for hurting your brother." Noah paused for a few seconds and then replied, "No... well, yes. How come I get in trouble for hitting my brother, but my mom doesn't get trouble for hitting me?" Good question.

You see, when Noah asked this question he was trying to make sense of the limit "no hitting" his parents set, no hitting; a reasonable limit. Being a concrete thinker, Noah understood not hitting another person as in "no hitting"—period. If he cannot hit his brother, why can he be hit? Even if you feel you have a good answer to this question, it won't work with Noah because as a concrete thinker, Noah can only understand this limit universally. If you think about it from Noah's perspective, he really does make a good point.

Okay, back to limit setting. Once you have stated the limit to your child and stated why you are setting it, there's still another step. Before I go on to the next step, I want to say a few things first "because I said so," or "because I am the parent, that's why," are not legitimate explanations to children for setting limits. Those responses insult the wisdom of children. Responses like that also communicate to your child that you are using your power as an adult without any good reason. This will not earn you respect or credibility. Without respect and credibility, the task of parenting becomes increasingly daunting. Plus, you know you promised yourself sometime around age ten that you would NEVER say that when you became a parent. There was a reason you felt that way; do not dismiss it.

Setting effective limits is one of the most difficult parenting skills. It takes practice to do it with expertise. You need to be patient with yourself as you make some adjustments, and also be patient with your children as they adjust too. Few parents have had a particular limit-setting structure to follow. It will take time to get used to following a structure and to shift from your former model and way of limit setting to this one. Limit setting is proactive because as a parent you are setting limits based on values and parenting principles rather than setting limits based on how you feel and your emotions. It can take a great deal of energy to change your focus, so you are demonstrating what you value versus how you feel.

It will also take some time for your child to adjust to your new style of limit setting. Although she may not have liked your old style, there was some consistency in that, and children crave consistency. You can count on some increased testing by your child of you and your new style of setting limits. Stick to the process here, to these parenting principles as well as your personal set of parenting principles, and you will pass the child's tests.

The final component to effective limit setting is telling children what they can do. Frequently, when we do set limits with our children, we tell them what they cannot do, but neglect to tell them what they can do. This is such an important piece of limit setting because children need help making good choices. It is often not clear from their perspective what would be a good choice in a particular situation. Let's take one last look at our limit list with all the components to limit setting in place. This is also a good time to refer back to Principle 4-Let me experience power and control by giving me choices (but don't overwhelm me).

"Don't talk to me that way, it is disrespectful. I am respectful to you. You can choose to change the way you are talking to me or choose to sit in time-out."
"Don't pick your nose, it is yucky. You can use a tissue and blow your nose."
"Don't say those words. I don't like hearing them or you saying them. You can use other words to tell me you're angry or even stomp your feet."
"Don't eat that with your fingers. I like you to use your good manners. You can use a fork."

### The Problem of a Tall Dad
Jason is a spirited five-year-old boy. He is skilled at testing his parents. One of the things he does that tests his parents' patience is standing on the furniture. When Jason's 6'6" dad comes home from work, Jason leaps onto the arm of the couch. He wants to be able to greet his dad face-to-face. He stands there and waits for Tall Dad to come through the door. Jason's mom tells him to get off the couch, she tells him it is bad manners, and it is disrespectful because the couch cost a lot of money. She yells at him, she picks him up and off the couch but he gets right back on. Tall Dad walks through the front door and finds Jason standing on the arm of the couch and his stressed wife yelling. Welcome home Tall Dad.

In Jason's defense, he is trying to solve the problem of not being able to greet his dad face-to-face. He loves his father like nobody's business and starts getting excited about Dad coming home an hour prior, when Tall Dad calls home and says he is leaving work. Then Mom, who also loves Tall Dad and is excited he is coming home from work, yells at him. There's turmoil and bad feelings when Tall Dad arrives home, but everyone wants him home, and he wants to be there—that's confusing.

Jason's parents needed a better way to set limits with Jason. What they were doing was not working. Here was the script we created. "Jason, you cannot stand on the couch. It is unsafe. If you want to be big like Daddy when he gets home, I can pick you up or you can stand on the stool."

When you communicate limits to your child, start off by using his name, and then set the limit in a clear and even-tempered way. Stating the child's name gets his attention. Children will listen to you because they feel safe even though a limit is being set if you say it without sounding upset. This particular style of limit setting works like a charm in child counseling and play therapy; that's where I learned it. I became a parent after I was trained as a child counselor and play therapist, and since I was clueless about how to limit my children, I used what I knew worked professionally. Surprise! It worked at home too! My teacher friends tell me it even works in the classroom.

**Your Turn**
How about you give it a try? That's the spirit! I'll give you a situation. You fill in the blanks. You've got this! Here's one more example, then you do it.
Andrea, you cannot give the cat candy because it could hurt him. You can give him a kitty treat. Thank you for cooperating.

(Name)_____, you cannot (Event)_____because (Reason)_____
You can (Acceptable Behavior)_____.Thank you for cooperating.


*Caring for children is a dance between setting appropriate limits as caretakers and avoiding un-*
*necessary power struggles that result in unhappiness.*
*Charlotte Davis Kasl, psychologist & author*

Principle #7

Provide me with consistency and stability
even if our life is chaotic.

*Our children are counting on us to provide two things: consistency and structure. Children need parents who say what they mean, mean what they say, and do what they say they are going to do.*
*Barbara Coloroso, speaker & author*

I have been a mental health counselor for twenty-five years. During that time, I have worked in a variety of settings with people aged eighteen months to eighty years old. They have been people in extreme poverty and teenagers with trust funds worth millions of dollars. The common theme in each and every client I have ever seen, regardless of the other differences, drastic or minimal, is their life is inconsistent and unstable. I consider it preventative medicine to provide your child with consistency and stability. When you are consistent, your children know what to expect. People do better in all areas of their lives when they know what to expect. It gives them a special kind of knowledge and comfort.

It is very difficult to provide your child consistency and stability in a chaotic world. However, it is the simple consistencies that will keep your child healthy, grounded, and well-adjusted. Stability promotes a parent-child relationship that's based in trust. Children can trust you to say and do what you say; and to be true to your word. Trust is the foundation of all strong relationships.

**Sleepover Night**
My children, like their mother, are not good sleepers. Neither of my children slept through the night by themselves until they were almost four (four years, not four months!). I will never write that parenting book on how to get your baby to sleep through the night.

My daughter, Leah, is our oldest child. At around age three, my husband and I were trying to problem solve because Leah was still not making it through the night on her own. She would wake up after midnight and call for us or come get us to lay down with her. We were tired.

We devised a plan and discussed it with Leah. When she could go the entire week, we showed her what this looked like on a calendar, sleeping through the night by herself, we would celebrate by having family sleepover night. Family sleepover night was to be held on Friday. We would pull out the sleeper sofa, get all our blankets and pillows set up and all three of us would sleep in the den.

Last night was Friday, and even though Leah is almost a teenager and we have Andrew (age eight) too, we had sleepover night like we have almost every Friday for the last nine years.

Because my children so love the consistency of sleepover night, it also has become a tool of negotiation. If you don't finish cleaning your room like I asked, no sleepover night. If you and your brother cannot problem solve who gets to choose what show to watch, no sleepover night. For my children, there is no sacrifice great enough to give up sleepover night. My children even consider sleepover night when deciding whether to accept or reject invitations to stay overnight at a friend's house. They typically will go so far as to negotiate a switch from Friday night to Saturday night. They don't want to miss it; they count on it.

This is going to sound strange, but you have to be flexible with your consistency. Like in the sleepover night story, you have to have some flexibility with your consistency. If one way you maintain stability for your children is to always have dinner at five thirty and a conflict in a family member's schedule emerges, how will you handle this? This should also be consistent. For example, if someone in our family has to get up super early the day after sleepover night, we either change to Saturday night or that person opts out. That might not sound like a great plan. However, when you know that next Friday there is another sleepover night, it's not a big deal.

Many of our family lives are chaotic for a variety of reasons that sometimes have to do with us as parents. Our work schedules, divorce/separation and visitation, economic hardship, emergencies, and commitments to others all can make providing consistency difficult. Sometimes it's connected to our children that our family life has gotten destabilized. There's a school play and your child has to stay after for practice, a new sport season, or changing from an elementary school to a middle school schedule are all child-centered destabilizers.

The trick is this: find a few things you can be consistent about and be as unwavering about that commitment as possible. You are making a commitment to your family, your child(ren) and yourself. Consistency provides children with a sense of predictability in a fast and ever-changing world. Consistency stabilizes children. When children have a sense of stability, they feel better, and therefore behave better.

Inconsistency, instability, and chaos on the other hand make behaving difficult for children. It's difficult to know what do to and how to do it when things are unpredictable. It's like being in a game where the rules keep changing. You feel confused and discouraged. We don't want our children to feel that way.

*Children are unpredictable.*
*You never know what inconsistency they're going to catch you in next.*
*Franklin P. Jones, reporter & humorist*

The following is a list of twenty simple ideas to keep consistency and stability. You'll notice that most of the ideas on the list, like sleepover night, do not have a monetary cost. They may be seasonal (we have particular consistencies during professional football season, for example), daily, weekly, etc. Regardless of what and how often, what you choose to do to provide consistency and stability for your children should be well-suited to your values, principles, and strengths as a parent. If you are not sure what your values and principles as a parent are, I suggest you do a web search for a "list of values and principles," and then find five of them you feel very connected to when you think about how you would like to parent.

Another way to do this is to ask people you are close with who have witnessed your parenting (this includes your children) to share with you what they have observed in terms of what is important to you as a parent. Make sure you thank anyone who is willing to be authentic and honest for the priceless feedback. Once you have read the list of examples here, write down five things you can do to bring some additional consistency and stability to your family and children.

You'll want to give it at least six to eight weeks to make an impact. You'll have to be patient (as it turns out, this is a great strength to develop as a parent). Your sticking to this is so important and directly connected with Principle 15 Be a man or woman of your word.

1.   Bedtime story
2.   Before school cuddle time
3.   Sit down breakfast
4.   Sunday dinner
5.   Weekend brunch
6.   Love note in school lunch
7.   Kiss goodnight
8.   Coloring time Saturday mornings
9.   Walk or bike ride after dinner on Fridays
10.  Homemade pizza night
11.  Game night
12.  Visiting with Grandma once a week on Saturday mornings
13.  Church, synagogue, mosque
14.  Clean room day
15.  Shower or bath schedule
16.  Stay in pajamas day
17.  Snack time after school
18.  Playtime after school
19.  One-on-one time (One parent, one child, NO interruptions. I suggest a minimum of fifteen to thirty minutes per week).
20.  Designated quiet time for reading, meditation, etc.

*I like consistency. If you've had a childhood like mine, you want some things*
*you can rely on to stay the same.*
*Norman Wisdom, actor & film producer*

Principle #8

Talk to me.

*If you talk to your children, you can help them to keep their lives together.*
*If you talk to them skillfully, you can help them to build future dreams.*
*Jim Rohn, entrepreneur & motivational speaker*

Children can read your non-verbal communications. It's like you are playing a constant game of charades. Not surprisingly then, they know what you are feeling and sometimes thinking. As children, especially young children, they might not have the words to demonstrate they are listening to you. What children understand from listening develops before, way before, what they can describe in words.

This is where talking to your children makes an impact. Talking to them, beginning at infancy (if not before they are even born), provides them with the words they will need to talk, with you and others, as they develop. More importantly, talking to your children demonstrates to them that you want to have a connection with them. It also allows them to get a sense of what is important to you and to your family.

Your child's receptive vocabulary (meaning the words they recognize and understand) develops at a faster pace than their expressive vocabulary (the words they use when speaking). This means that when you are talking to your children, they understand before they can articulate that they can understand. They are building a vast vocabulary even if they aren't using it—yet.

There are some things you definitely want to talk to your children about.
Your children love to hear about other members of their family and close network. They like to hear what you are doing as you are doing it, like house cleaning, cooking, or exercising. You are, in essence, sharing your world with them. Even very young children appreciate this. It is important to remember that children, for the most part, are egocentric, meaning they believe they are at the center of the world—your world. This is developmentally normal. When you talk to your children, connect it to them and their perspective; you are playing into their egocentrism, which will make them more interested in what you are talking about. You are creating the building blocks for good listening skills.

There are some things you definitely do NOT want to talk to your children about. The children I have been blessed to have as clients in my mental health counseling practice are to be thanked for this lesson. Many times, they have either talked or played out communications from parents that leave them feeling anxious, vulnerable, confused, and/or angry.

You have to be thoughtful with what you talk to your child about. If you do not want certain topics to be discussed or language to be used, do not model talking about such topics or using those words for your child.

Here are some additional suggestions of topics that have come up either directly or indirectly from the children I see in counseling. They want you to talk to them—just not about this stuff.

1. Do not talk about their other parent regardless of the nature of your relationship with that person.

2. Do not talk about your emotional problems or issues.

3. Do not talk about your negative view of yourself (Moms PLEASE don't put down your body in front of your daughters).

4. Do not talk about your sexual experiences past and present (It's not appropriate and it grosses your children out).

5. Do not talk about subjects that might scare your child.

It also is helpful if you can think back to your childhood. Can you recall awkward or disturbing conversations with your parents? What were the topics of those conversations? What about the topics which caused your discomfort? What do you wish your parents did differently? The answers to those questions will give you great information about what you should do.

## Chris uses foul language

At age seven, Chris had been through a great deal and was currently in foster care. He was removed from the custody of his biological parents, for neglect. His parents were struggling with domestic violence, drug use, and extreme poverty. Chris was not safe. He was exposed to all of this. His parents were so unavailable to his needs that he often went without his basic needs met. This included Chris being sexually abused while his parents were in the other room, unable to provide safety for him because of their own troubles.

Chris had an incredibly colorful vocabulary. I am not one who is typically thrown off by strong language, but Chris found a way to make me blush. I was somewhat impressed, as strange as that sounds, with the sophistication of the swear words he used in our play therapy sessions. He was particularly skilled at stringing profanity together in unique and powerful sentences.

Chris' parents worked very hard on their individual recovery from alcohol and other drugs. They took parenting classes, went for individual counseling, participated in family counseling, and voluntarily participated in a home-based parenting aide program. They impressed all the service providers with their hard work. Chris was looking forward to reuniting with his parents. At a team meeting, which included myself and the other human service professionals, Chris' parents, and foster care parents, Chris' foster mom made a comment about the words she heard Chris use with me during our play therapy sessions There are two important things I should mention here: 1) in play therapy, children are allowed to use any words they choose, 2) Chris would yell those colorful words, so even with the door closed and a sound machine on to disguise what was being said, it was still apparent. Chris' parents were shocked that he would use such foul language and his father said, "I don't know why he would say those words. Only the adults in our home can talk that way." The words you use with and around your child are the cornerstone of the language they will use.

In many families, there are words (mannerisms and gestures too) that the adults can use, and a separate set of words that are permitted for children to say. Children view adults as people who have power. Even the words adults use have power. Power is alluring to children who typically feel powerless. You can be sure if you use those powerful words in front of your children that they will use those powerful words as well. The truth is that they will hear, learn, and then use those powerful words even if you do not use them in your home. If you don't use those words in your home, then you can say to your children, "In our home we don't use those words. That means all of us." You can then set a consequence for your child if she uses that word again. "If you use that word again, you will lose your TV time for one day." If the adults in your home do use that language, you can still specify to your child that some words are only for adults to use and set consequences just the same. The foundation, however, of your reasoning is shaky and children are usually pretty good at illuminating that.

*Just talking to your child is only half the job. You can keep the lines of communication*
*open by knowing how to listen and when to talk.*
*National Youth Anti-Drug Media Campaign*

As indicated in the quote above, it's not just knowing what to say, but when to say it that is important when talking to your child. In order to get the fullest parenting potential out of this principle, I offer you some guidelines. Again, these guidelines come from children themselves.

1.      Pay close attention to the body language and facial expressions of your children as you are talking. If they seem distracted or disinterested, that's because they are. Let whatever it was you were talking to them about go (unless you were setting a limit).

2.      Use clear and concrete language.

3.      Keep your sentences short.

4.      Do not lecture or preach.

5.      Let them interrupt with their stories or questions. I know that may sound like the opposite of what you would think would work. However, the reason is that if they are interrupting or asking questions, that means they are not only listening to what you are saying but also processing it.

6.      Do not try and talk to them when they are tired or out of sorts. No one listens well in that state.

7.      Do not talk to them when they are engaged in another activity, even watching television or playing a video game. You cannot compete with that level of stimulation. You will need to shut down the TV, computer, etc., if you want to talk to your child.

8.      **Do** talk to them over a meal.

9.      **Do** talk to them face-to-face.

10.     **Do** talk to them about how much you love them.

*There's nothing that can help you understand your beliefs*
*more than trying to explain them to an inquisitive child.*
*Frank A. Clark, newspaper cartoonist*

# Principle #9

## Show me it is ok to make mistakes.

*When you make a mistake, admit it.*
*If you don't, you only make matters worse.*
*Ward Cleaver, character from the TV show Leave it to Beaver*

Many of the mental health problems adolescents and adults display in counseling are connected to the illusion that they must be perfect. Adolescents and adults have all sorts of ways of deciding what "perfect" is. I have heard a range of explanations of perfection. Some believe perfection is being a certain size or weight, having a particular job, earning a specific salary, or having a position on a team. These beliefs about how perfection is manifested do not come from our imagination. These beliefs that we can, and therefore should be perfect come from the myths we believed as children. I am talking about the adult perpetuated myths whose themes are perfection.

### Bunny Ears and Sneakers

Before I get into this story, I have a few confessions I need to make to you. The first is that I have personally struggled with perfectionism. It is only within the last ten years that I have opted for excellence versus perfection. Second, I am not skilled at tying shoelaces. Mine do not stay tied unless I make a double knot. That was liberating; thanks for listening and being accepting of me, now on with the story.

My daughter and I were preparing for a day out of the house. We had errands to run and we were going to eat lunch with some of our friends. At age three, Leah already had a sense of her style. She wanted to wear a pair of new shoes that had laces. These were her first laced shoes. Up until this point, we had loved the Velcro closures. I tied her shoes, telling her what I was doing as I made the bunny ears with the laces, crisscrossed them and ta-da, her shoes were tied. The tie lasted less than ten minutes. Leah pointed out as I helped her get out of the car, "Momma, my shoe is open even though you made the bunny ears tie." Ugh. I tied her shoes again, this time with a double knot.
I said to her, "Leah I made a mistake when I tied your shoes. It didn't work. I got the tie wrong." She paused as if frozen for a few seconds then said in a surprised tone, "Momma, you made a mistake?"
"Yes, Leah, I did. I make mistakes ALL the time." She laughed.

Later at lunch with our friends Leah greeted each of the other moms with, "My mom made a mistake today." How cute. During lunch, I dropped my fork. "Momma, you made another mistake."
"Yes, Leah, even Mommas drop things." I pronounced my friend's daughter's name, Dawn, with my Long Island, New York accent.
Leah noticed, "Momma, you made another mistake. It's Dawn not DAUNA." Thanks for the tip, Leah.

For another week or two, all of my mistakes were pointed out by my three-year-old. I'll tell you something; it was great. She learned two important lessons, that her momma wasn't perfect and that grown-ups make mistakes. I learned an important lesson too: my child loves me even with all my imperfections.

As parents, we want to set the example that making mistakes is a way of learning. We want to show that we accept ourselves with our imperfections. We have to show this, not just say it. Remember, children listen through watching and not just listening. As parents, we cannot accept our children's mistakes until we accept ourselves including our mistakes. Make a list of all your mistakes that you are holding on to. I bet some of them are even from your childhood. Write them down or create a document on your computer. Once you have exhausted your mistake memory, purge it. Say aloud to yourself, "I forgive you for your mistakes." Then destroy the list (my favorite way is to run over it with my car repeatedly). If you put it on paper or you made an electronic list, trash and delete it forever. Remember children listen through watching and not just listening.

Inspirational author and presenter, Deepok Chopra refers to making mistakes this way, "Failures are the seeds of success." Chopra knows what he is talking about. Making mistakes often doesn't just offer a lesson, but has hidden positives. Here are ten inventions that were made by mistake:
1. Penicillin
2. Chocolate Chip Cookies
3. Potato Chips
4. The Pacemaker
5. Silly Putty
6. Microwave Ovens
7. The Slinky
8. Fireworks
9. Corn Flakes Cereal
10. Post-it Notes

Show your child that you make mistakes and that you learn from them. There are some dangers that are connected to not owning up to your mistakes that go beyond carrying the torch for perfectionism. Not admitting your mistakes gets in the way of relationships with your children. Parents who are not honest with their mistakes set the stage for children who will struggle with perfectionism, trust, and connection. It's difficult to feel connected and trust a person who is not honest with you or themselves about their mistakes.


Some reasons to show your child that you make mistakes:
• It demonstrates that you accept yourself, which makes it much more likely that they believe you will be accepting of them regardless of their imperfections.
• It shows that you can learn from mistakes.
• It shows you can laugh at yourself and have a good sense of humor.
• Making mistakes means you are okay with not always being right.
• Making mistakes demonstrates you don't always have to win.
• When you illuminate your mistakes to your children they learn that adults are not always perfect or right. This may help keep your child from trusting adults who do not deserve their trust.
• You highlight that making mistakes is not a big deal. This minimizes your child's

fears about your finding out about the mistakes he or she has made. Children who are afraid of what will happen if their imperfections are found out tend to lie (because they are scared, not because they are bad).

One of the surest ways to curb anxiety and depression in your child well beyond his or her child-hood years is to model mistake-making. You will have plenty of opportunities to make mistakes; that's what parents do.

> *Mistakes are part of the dues one pays for a full life.*
> *Sophia Loren, actress*

Principle #10

Don't stop showing me affection even as I grow up.

*Your children need your presence more than your presents.*
*Jesse Jackson, civil rights activist & Baptist minister*

Teagan is a precocious, smart, and athletic thirteen-year-old. She was referred to counseling because she was feeling sad, lacked self-confidence, and was making poor choices in social relationships. Specifically, Teagan was using her phone to exchange provocative sexual texts and photos with boys.

Teagan easily engaged with me in counseling. The girl I met was talkative, spunky, and outgoing. In our very first counseling session, she shared how upset she had been since her uncle died two years ago and that her parent's recent divorce had been really tough emotionally for her. She also shared with me that she was grounded; she had her phone taken away for a week. I asked, "What could have happened that you got your phone taken away?" Teagan said, "I took pictures of myself and sent them to some boys. You know pictures of my private parts." Oh, those kinds of pictures. Yikes.

The following week, Teagan came in for her regularly scheduled session. She had her phone back. I remarked that she must be happy to have it back. She shrugged like she felt indifferent. That was a curious response to me. I commented, "It looks like you are not sure if you really want your phone back." She responded, "I think I am growing up too fast." She was; she knew it and needed help.

Teagan clearly had a lot going on and needed support. As she was growing up (she looked and acted older than thirteen), she said her parents had stopped hugging her and lying down with her at nighttime. She was able to state clearly that even though she was now a teenager, she still needed her parents to show her love. As part of her counseling, we created a list of what she thought would help so that we could later share it with her parents during a consultation.

Here is what Teagan came up with:

1.     Goodnight kisses
2.     Read to me
3.     Lay down with me at night
4.     Polish my nails
5.     Play with my hair
6.     Hug me goodbye when I leave for school
7.     Come to my sporting events and cheer me on
8.     Notice my good grades and brag about them to family members
9.     Lie down with me and watch TV
10.    Ask for passwords to my phone, facebook account, computer, etc.

That this teenager needed were her parents to do what they had done when she was a little girl—show her love. There was good news; her parents were happy to return to these overt acts of affection. Guess what happened? Teagan began to feel better and then made better choices.

Teagan's lesson is a powerful and important one: show your children affection even as they grow up. Different children have different affection needs. These needs may change as they grow up. Notice I said change; I did not say disappear.

**No More Goodbye Kisses**

I have affectionate children. They have always been cuddly. They enjoyed and shared random physical expressions of affection within our family. My son, Andrew has been known to give "Hug-a-bugga-hugs." This special version of a hug is reserved for only the most special people. The hug starts about ten feet away from the person to be hugged. Andrew runs and jumps into the lucky (and hopefully sturdy) person's arms and squeezes with all his little-boy might.

His sister is equally affectionate. Leah likes to cuddle. Our children typically give kisses of hello, goodbye, and thank you in our extended family. They give us kisses goodnight and expect kisses goodnight in return.

Then one day, something strange happened. Leah was going up to her room for the night. She said goodnight to me and gave me a kiss. She then said goodnight to her dad. No kiss. Instead she hugged him. Not a warm embrace, more like she was patting him on the back. What was that about?

What it was about with Leah, and will eventually be about with Andrew, is that the degree of physical affection they want from their parents diminishes to a degree in adolescence. This is directly connected to the maturation process of puberty. What this means is that your adolescent may pull away a bit from physical displays of affection within the family. This happens to a greater degree in front of their friends and peers.

This can be a confusing signal for us as parents. We may feel a sense of grief or loss, rejection or even fear. The true message though is not that our older child doesn't need or want our affection; it is that we need to show it differently. This is going to require some thoughtfulness on your part. Here are five ways of showing your affection to your older child:

1.      Write her a note saying you love her. Highlight something about them personally that you admire.
   An example is: "Hi Honey, I just wanted to say I love you and I appreciate how cooperative you were this morning. Love, Mom."
2.      Make him a special meal or treat. Illuminate that you did it because he is special and important to you.
3.      Give a side-to-side hug or a kiss on the head. They involve less physical touching although a physical affection can still be displayed and experienced.
4.      Send a text. Communicate on their terms.
How about: "I love u. Just wanted u 2 know."
5.      Ask for a parent date. Would your child be willing to go to the movies with you? How about movie night at home? What about baking cookies together or playing a game of miniature golf? The possibilities are endless.

*Out of all the things that we are supposed to do as parents,*
*showing our children affection and love is at the top of list.*
*Anita James*

## Principle #11

I'll do better in school when I feel better at home and about myself.

*You can get all A's and still flunk life.*
*Walker Percy, author*

Kenzi was eleven years old when her dad died in a car accident. She began counseling with me several months after the incident. Things had changed a lot since his death. Her mom was working more and not home after school until after dinnertime. Kenzi had to make herself dinner. The family home was too expensive without Dad's income, and Kenzi and her mom had moved into another home several miles from where she had grown up.

Kenzi had always been an outstanding student. She earned grades throughout elementary school in the high 90s. In fact, she had never earned anything less than a 96. She was the student her teachers could count on to understand and apply their lessons with vigor and enthusiasm. She loved school.

A few months into counseling and six months after her dad had died, Kenzi came to a session looking visibly upset. This was not characteristic of Kenzi. I inquired. Kenzi reported that she would not be able to sing in the chorus concert because of her grades. "What do you mean?" I asked "I thought you were an excellent student." Through her sobs she shared that she had a 64 in social studies and you had to have a 65 or better in all subjects to sing at the concert.

After the session, I spoke with Kenzi's mom who shared the same story. Her mom said she had even called the school in an attempt to have the rule bent for Kenzi. Mom said, "Really, she's only one point below in one subject. The kid's dad died less than a year ago." Mom was furious because the school official's reply was that there would be no exceptions. Mom also conveyed that she was upset with Kenzi too. Her grades had slipped incredibly this year, with her highest scores in the low 70s.

I learned from Kenzi (and many other amazing teachers who have come into my life as my counseling clients) that in order to learn, and do well in school, children need to have a home life that is safe and growth-promoting. Like Kenzi, other children have taught me that when there are problems and stresses at home, it is difficult (at best) to learn and flourish in school.

If you are like me and your child's school performance, measured by grades, is important to you, you do not have to abandon your values to follow this principle. What I am asking parents to do in practicing this principle is to really take an emotional health inventory of what is going on with their children.
Ask yourself (and if you don't know, ask your child):

- Has there been a major loss like death of a grandparent or family member?
- Have you recently moved?
- Did one your best friends move away?
- Did a close friendship fizzle out?

*Any of these losses would be a disruption that could get in the way of learning and school performance.*

- What is going on with how your child feels about himself?
- Did he get cut from the team?
- Does he have acne?
- Is she an early or late developer?
- Did something happen that has recently embarrassed him?

*If so, it would make sense that school performance would suffer.*

- What about at home; is there domestic violence?
- Is someone in the family suffering from addiction?
- Did an older sibling move away?

*Again, any of these home life issues may affect children's abilities to learn and flourish in school.*

These are just some examples. Think specifically about your child(ren). You are the expert when it comes to your child. What questions are missing from this list?

Problems at home also impact a child's self-esteem. Children who do not feel good about who they are, do not do well in school. If you think about it, why would they? If they did well, it would be in contrast to the negative way they already view themselves. People make decisions about who they are. This is true of children and adults. If your child has decided, "I am not that smart" or "I am not a good student," he or she will behave accordingly. There is a comfort and predictability in that. If your child then does well academically in school, he has to rethink his identity and reorganize his view of himself; that takes a great deal of emotional work. It is easier for children to stick with a negative view of self. I know that sounds strange, however, even adults do it. Have you ever lost or gained a significant amount of weight? When you navigate the world, do you do so at your current weight or at the weight you used to be at? Just as I thought: You see yourself at the former weight. It takes years and focus to make those types of perceptive adjustments.

It is easy to overlook some of the less drastic and subtle experiences that may interfere with our children doing well in school. If it is a big deal to your child, it will have a big impact. It does not matter so much what "it" is but how "it" is experienced.

## It's Not a Big Deal

LaShonda's grades had plummeted. She went from being an A student to being at risk of failing all her subjects. Her parents were confused and upset. LaShonda was blessed with a very good life. Her parents had absolutely no idea what could be going on with LaShonda. In fact, they were scared because they felt so helpless.

In counseling sessions with LaShonda, I learned about her home life and school. She also shared about her extended family and dance lessons. She was a pleasant, bright little girl. I was as clueless as her parents about why her school performance had changed so radically.

Then there was a clue. LaShonda said, "Hi" to another child in the waiting area on the way into her counseling session. She said, "That's Tracy from school: she's nice to me."
I commented, "Tracy is your friend."
LaShonda looked down and said, "I don't have friends because I was the teacher's pet."
I asked directly, "So you don't have friends because the teacher likes you?"
LaShonda said, "Now I do, bad grades. I want to have friends."

I shared this exchange with her parents who were aware that other children were referring to her as the "teacher's pet." LaShonda's mom said, "That's it? We didn't think that was a big deal." It was to LaShonda. Her parents rallied around her and supported her in developing friendships while still being a good student. They did not minimize her experience or tell her to get over it. They recognized that it was a big deal to LaShonda, a very big deal.

It's not just negative events and stress that can affect academic performance. Sometimes positive events and experiences can also get in the way of learning and academic performance. Events like a new baby in the family, Mom returning home from deployment, or moving to a new house can all be so exciting and distracting for children that focus in school and on homework become nearly impossible.

The good news is that we, as parents, can really have an impact here on our children and on their academic performance in school. If we follow the other principles in this book, we are doing, and more importantly, being what our children need in order to combat the fallout from difficulties at home and stresses to their self-esteem.

Principle #12

Let's Play!

*Play keeps us fit physically and mentally.*
*Stuart Brown, professor of psychiatry*

Children communicate and learn through play. Play is considered the work of childhood because children develop socially, emotionally, cognitively, and physically through play.

As a mental health counselor with specialized training in play therapy, it may not be surprising that "Let's Play" is one of the twenty principles for being the parent your child needs. What may surprise you is that playing with my children is a principle that I have to work hard at incorporating. I think it's important that you know that even as a credentialed play therapist, playing with my children takes practice and intention. I am sold on this importance of play; it is the practice of it, making time for it, that I struggle with. If, after twenty-five years of being a play therapist I still have to put effort into playing with my children, you can cut yourself some slack if playing with your children does not come easily to you.

## What Makes Playing so Difficult for Parents?

One of the things I have observed in myself, and in my counseling and play therapy students, is that many of us don't really know how to play. Maybe we did some time ago, but now, we have forgotten. The good news is this: even if you forgot how to play, your child can reconnect you to play. Follow the lead of your child in play and it will come back to you. If you were a child who was not playful, your child can teach you how to be playful. It is a blessing to us, and our children, for our children to have opportunities to be the expert at something (in this case, play), especially in their relationship with their parents. It's crucial for children to feel like they are good at something. It helps build their sense of self and self-esteem. Children are typically experts at playing. Allow them this opportunity to teach you something and feel good about themselves and you while they do it.

Some adults have difficulty playing because their childhood experiences did not honor the importance of play or provide them with opportunities for playing. Some childhoods are that empty. I can tell you from my professional experience, that even children who have lived in situations where there is severe neglect and abuse can usually play. What that means is if you missed out on playing as a child because of the nature of your childhood, there is still a playful child inside of you. As adults, we tend to value productive time and do not consider play as such. It is though! The benefits of play are numerous. Perhaps most importantly as parents we need to recognize that play is a relationship-building activity. Make time for it.

Adults who have a difficult time connecting or reconnecting to the playfulness of childhood may want to try any or all of these activities to appreciate the awesomeness of play.

    1.     Color with crayons.
    2.     Spin around and around until you get dizzy. Even ask another person to have a spinning contest with you. See who can spin the longest.

3.    Head to your backyard or the local park. Slide down the slide and swing on the swings.
4.    Skip.
5.    Finger paint with pudding.

## A little bit about what happens in play therapy

Children communicate through their play (see the story: Our little Leah is cute, but strange, Principle 5, Listen to Me) so child therapy that is play-based makes sense intuitively. Using play therapy with children allows child and counselor a means of communicating that does not rely solely on verbal communication. In play therapy, children do not even have to talk for therapy and healing to happen because they are communicating through their play. It's very cool and rewarding to have play therapy relationships with children. My experiences playing with children as a play therapist have taught me about the importance of parents playing with children.

> *You will always be your child's favorite toy.*
> *Vicki Lansky, Trouble-Free Travel with Children*

Children clients love play therapy and playing with me. They typically do not want to leave when their session is over and even say they want to come every day. Without minimizing the power of play therapy and the relationship between child and play therapist, the truth is your child would much rather play with you, their parent.

## Can mommy come into the playroom?

Beth and her mom had been separated for four months while Beth was in foster care and her mom was at an inpatient drug rehabilitation program. The first five years of Beth's life were chaotic and scary. She had been neglected and abused. Although she was five years old, she was not fully potty trained, she did not know her ABCs, and she lagged behind her peers, socially, emotionally, and cognitively.

I had been seeing Beth for play therapy the entire time she was in foster care. When Beth's mom had successfully completed the recovery program, the service providers were confident that Beth and her mother could be reunified and that Beth could be safe and have opportunities to thrive. Beth began to visit with her mom more frequently, and her mom took over the responsibility of bringing her to her counseling appointments.

Beth asked if her mom could play with us as part of our play therapy session. I was reluctant. I wanted to meet with Beth's mom prior to make sure she understood play ther- apy, that she could help Beth's healing process, and that she would not use the session to meet her needs; that didn't happen. I allowed Beth's mom to come in without having a consultation because I wanted to honor Beth advocating and asserting herself.

What did happen, however, was really amazing. Beth told her mom how the play therapy room worked. Basically, she got to play what she wanted and how she wanted. I winked at Beth's mom and said, "Beth is the boss in here, except when she needs help being safe. You can just play with her; she'll show you what you need to do." Beth's mom smiled and inside I grew increasingly concerned. This was a woman who had so many limits; she had her mental health issues, she just got out of drug and alcohol recovery treatment, she had a limited education, and lived in poverty. After about five minutes of watching Beth and her mom play together, I was no longer worried. In fact, I was in awe of Beth's mom.

Beth pretended she was a baby and rather than reprimand her daughter for using baby talk,

Beth's mom cuddled her. She used baby talk back, smiled at and rocked "baby Beth" in her arms. Beth said, "Change my diaper." Mom pretended to change her diaper. Beth ordered, "Feed me." Her mom found the baby bottle and pretended to feed her.

Beth's mom turned to me and said, "I did not do this right the first time; she's giving me a second chance." Beth's mom realized that her child's play was a communication and an opportunity. The three of us met for several more sessions, each time Beth invited her mother in. I became an observer and witness; Beth no longer wanted me to be an active player. The willingness of Beth's mom to play, led to the smooth transition of Beth's custody back to her mom.

I am going to offer some suggestions about playing with your child. Some of these suggestions are probably things you are already doing (Yes! Good for you.). I also will give you some ideas that may sound strange, or impossible or go against what you thought you were supposed to do as a parent. I am asking that you take a leap of faith and trust me. I truly want for you and your child to have an amazing relationship based in love and respect. I will not steer you wrong.

## It's playtime

- When possible, play with your child should be spontaneous.
- When being spontaneous is not yours nor your child's strength, schedule playtime (a minimum of twenty minutes/week—that may sound like hardly any time at all, but the truth is most children get a lot less than that, if any).
- Put scheduled playtime on the calendar where your child can reference it (use a symbol or picture if they are not able to read words yet).
- Only true emergencies are reasons for rescheduling playtime.
- Interruptions are not allowed during special playtime (turn your phone on silent, for example). Plan ahead to so that the possibility of interruptions can be minimized.
- Allow your child to lead the play. She decides what to play and how to play it. Do not let the structure of games be the focus; this includes allowing your child to make up the rules of games and to decide whether she will actually stick to the rules.
- Be attentive to your child. Get down on your child's level physically and make eye contact.
- Allow your child to solve problems during the play. Do not rush in to fix things or show him how certain toys work. Only help him when he asks or cues you that he wants your help.
- Allow your child to make mistakes during play and do not correct mistakes.
- Recognize that your child is communicating to you through play. Your child is showing you her perspective. Be attentive to how she sees the world so that you can empathize and understand her point of view.
- You do not have to directly teach your child anything during play. He is learning when he plays. When you try to teach him something during play it interrupts the natural flow and fun of play.
- Be playful and silly—enjoy yourself and your child.

And with tweens and teens? Playtime shifts to activity time. You will want to maintain the same philosophy as above. With older children, however, rather than playing you may be watching a movie, shopping, taking a walk, or going for a swim.

*Play is our brain's favorite way of learning.*
*Diane Ackerman, author & poet*

Principle #13

Ask for my feedback.

*Feedback is the breakfast of champions.*
*Ken Blanchard, author*

I have some questions for you: On a scale of 1-10 (1 being awful and 10 being excellent) how good of a parent do you think you are? How do you know this? What types of feedback do you get about your parenting? Who do you get it from? If you are not a 10, what would make you a 10? Are you willing to do what it takes to be a 10?

Get ready for this: I want you to ask your child for feedback about your parenting and to use this feedback to make decisions about the kind of parent you want to be to your child. Speaking of this, what kind of parent do you want to be to your child? Take some time to reflect on how you felt when your child entered your life. Think about all the prayers and promises you made relating to the health and welfare of your child. Write down five descriptive words that serve as the foundation for the type of parent you wanted to be then.

Next, write down five descriptive words that describe the type of parent you are now.

Compare the lists.

What action steps can you take to be the parent you had originally dreamed of being, keeping in sync with your prayers and promises?

*Loving a baby is a circular business, a kind of feedback loop.*
*The more you give, the more you get, and the more you get, the more you feel like giving.*
*Penelope Leach, psychologist*

In Jack Canfield's book The Success Principles, he discusses the importance of feedback. He shares with the readers the very question I started this chapter off with, "On a scale of 1-10…" According to Canfield he learned this question and the importance of the follow-up question (What would make it a 10?). This assessment can be used in any aspect of your life—personal or professional. For our purposes, we are going to use it to find out about our parenting.

## I'm a solid 9

I think I am a good parent. I am thoughtful about how I parent my children, and I reflect on my successes as well as my mistakes (there are many of both). I decided I would ask my children how they would rate me. I thought a good time to ask would be when I go in to give each one of them a kiss goodnight. Guess what happened when I was about to ask them? I chickened out!!! I got nervous that I might not like their answers, that they would think I sucked as a parent, that I had ruined their childhoods.

About a week later I was able to muster up some courage. I reread Canfield's chapter on feedback. I wanted this information from my kids and I needed it in order to have an accurate understanding of their perspectives. There was no way I could improve my parenting without it. I am sharing this with you because I want you to know that I would not ask you to do something that I am not willing to do myself. Here is what I found out.

I am a 9. My daughter, who was ten years old at the time, rated me a 9. What did I need to do to be a 10 in her eyes? Easy, work less. I had a feeling I was going to get some feedback about my schedule. My son, who was six years old the first time I posed the feedback question, responded with, "You're weird." He then also rated me a 9.
"What would make me a 10?" I asked.
"Don't yell so much." What? Yell? I don't yell. I may raise my voice and say things sternly, but I most certainly do not yell. From my son's perspective, I yell. Crap—I don't want to be a yeller. I know yelling doesn't work.

As it turns out I got great feedback from my children. I figured out how to squeeze out even a little more time to be with them rather than working. I also monitored my volume when I was irritated and angry.

I check in several times a year with my children since that original check-in about my parenting. I learn something about how my children view me, what is important to them and how I can be a better mom each time.

One more thing, you also will get feedback from your children about your parenting when they play and draw. When they play out the role of the parent in spontaneous play, how do they play? Are they nurturing? Do they play a "mean dad?" Do they reprimand or criticize? All this gives you information about how they see you. Sometimes this also comes out in drawings. Below is an example. My daughter, at five years old, drew this picture of our family without any instruction. You can see she labeled each of us by name and used a word to describe each person, including herself.

Yes, that's me… Angry Mom. How's that for some feedback? I am guessing *I was yelling* more than I thought. I'll be honest. When I first looked at her drawing, I could feel myself get upset; mostly hurt and embarrassed. I started saying things to myself like, "You are a bad parent, you get angry so easily, you're awful, why does Daddy get to be silly and I'm angry?" As you can guess saying these things to myself is what was making me feel horrible. What this drawing was, was feedback. I can take action when I get, and listen to feedback. And that's exactly what I did, took action. I made sure that I showed my children a fuller range of my feelings. I stopped barking orders about cleaning up, and I found ways to show them that although I am not as silly as Daddy, I have a silly side too. Ask for feedback and then incorporate it. It's hard work that will result in an improved relationship between you and your child. You and your child deserve that.

Principle #14

Read to me.

*Children are made readers on the laps of their parents.*
*Emilie Buchwald, Author*

There is a great deal of research that has demonstrated the importance of parents reading to their children. It helps children become readers early on and for life. You might be thinking, "That's nice and everything but why should it be a parenting principle; surely there are other aspects of parenting that are more important?"

Reading to your child has benefits for the child-parent relationship that go way beyond your child's ability to learn how to read and become an avid reader. When you read to your child, many things are happening.

When you read to your child she has your attention. Although you are focused on reading the book, your child is only somewhat focused on the story. She is watching and listening to you. She is learning all about you as a person. She learns how you use your voice to communicate certain emotions. She learns what you sound like when you are the villain and when you are the hero. She learns what your face looks like when you are reading about being afraid or being brave. She learns about communication with you because she is seeing and hearing how your tone varies, how your face changes, how the volume of your voice gets softer and louder. All of this benefits your relationship because she learns how to read, not the book, but you.

Any behavior or way of being that strengthens the parent-child relationship is of value to our parenting. Reading is one of those behaviors. Children experience being read to as an act of nurturance by the reader. When we read to children, they feel cared about.

**A class of graduate students**
A few years ago, I decided to begin my "Introduction to Play Therapy" course by reading my students a children's book. The students in this particular class ranged in age from twenty-two years old to forty-seven years old. The reason I wanted to read them this book was to help get them in the mindset of being a child. If they could do that, my hypothesis was then they could better relate to their future clients in play therapy. I was a little nervous that they would feel insulted or like I was being disrespectful by reading a children's book to them. I asked for written feedback about the class activities that we did that day. They were not required to include their names with the feedback.

Surprise, surprise. Each student indicated that their favorite part of class that day was having the story read to them. More than half indicated that they hoped I would read to them again. One student said, "I thought I might cry while you were reading to us even though it wasn't a sad story. I just felt so cared for." If this was the experience of graduate students having their professor stand in the front of the classroom reading them a book, imagine how your child feels.

Now imagine how this feels to your child, if as you read to him, he is sitting on your lap or cuddled up next to you. The nurturance experience is even more outstanding. If he feels cared for when being read to, the physical proximity communicates warmth, caring, trust, safety, and love.

### The little boy who threw a chair at his teacher

Many of the children I provide counseling for are referred for aggressive behaviors. Paul was one of these children. At five years old and in kindergarten, he had been suspended twice. He had punched a classmate in the stomach and had stabbed another child with a pencil. He had just been expelled from school for throwing a chair at his teacher when I started working with him.

Paul had witnessed a great deal of violence in his home. His father had been incarcerated as a result and his mother was hospitalized for ongoing mental health issues. She could not take care of Paul. Paul was in foster care.

In his play therapy sessions, Paul often played out aggressive and violent scenes. He was never physically aggressive toward me, however, in anyway. One day he came into the play therapy room and asked if I had any books. I remarked, "You don't want to play with the toys today." He said, "Can you read to me?" We went and found a book from the waiting area that was appropriate for his age and looked interesting to him.

We sat across from each other on the floor and I began reading. He was intently listening and watching me. When I made eye contact with him, he smiled. About a page or two into the book he asked tentatively, "Jodi, can I sit in your lap when you read?"
If Paul was my child that would have been an easy, "of course." Paul, though, is my client and I practice having good boundaries. I did not want to create dependency in Paul or confuse him about the limits of our relationship. I responded, "You can come right here next to me." He did.

After I completed the book he said, "I want to do that every time, every time!
We can play after the story." That's what we did for weeks. I read to him, then he engaged in the play therapy session.

One day while I was reading to him, Paul turned to me and said, "I love when you read to me. You look beautiful like a princess." That's quite a comment from a little boy who had displayed such aggression and violence in other settings.
"Paul, you really love when I read to you."
He replied, "It's my favorite thing in the whole world. It makes me want to be good." My eyes filled with tears, my face with a smile, and my heart with sunshine as this troubled little boy felt like a loved little boy because someone read to him.

Sometimes reading to our children can be a test in patience. We get excited to read a particular book and then our little one does not pay attention. You choose a book that was one of your own when you were a child and your child turns the pages before you can finish reading what's on the page. As you are reading in your best character voices, keeping up with the perfect rhythm of the story, your child keeps interrupting and asking questions. These behaviors can be such annoyances to us that we don't want to read. They can make reading to your child stressful. This is not your child trying to annoy you or get you aggravated. This is about your child being interested in what you are doing and reading. These behaviors may test your patience and you must pass the test! I'm going to give you some clues about how to pass the test:
1.      Read with enthusiasm.

2.    Read about things your child is interested in.

3.    Let your child pick the book even if she chooses the same one day after day (repetition is a key to learning).

4.    If she wants to turn the pages, let her. You can read the book word by word another time. Make up parts of the story that you cannot read because she turned the pages.

5.    If he wants to turn the pages and you are afraid he will rip them, stick with board books until this is no longer an issue.

6.    Take breaks to make eye contact during the story.

7.    Take breaks to kiss or hug your child during the story.

8.    As your child develops into a reader ask them to read a few words or an entire page.

9.    Make up silly answers to the questions he asks as you tell the story.

10.    Ask your child questions about the story like, "Which was your favorite monster?" or "Did you think the princess looks like me?"

Reading to, and with your child is a journey based in connection.

> *The more you read, the more things you will know.*
> *The more that you learn, the more places you'll go.*
> *Dr. Seuss, "I Can Read With My Eyes Shut!"*

Be a person of your word.

*Promises are the uniquely human way of ordering the future,*
*making it predictable and reliable to the extent that this is humanly possible.*
*Hannah Arendt, political theorist*

Children are natural accountability holders. By this I mean, if you tell your child you will do something, you better be prepared to do it. If you make a promise, you have to keep it. This is true not for just positive promises like "I promise to buy you that toy." It is as important when the promise is disciplinary "If you do not brush your teeth right now, you will not go to the sleepover party tomorrow." They will hold you accountable by testing if you will be a man or woman of your word.

Being a person of your word is a key element to parenting. It establishes trust. If you say you are going to do something and then you do not, children make sense of that as a betrayal of trust. Without follow-through, your word, promises, and threats become meaningless to your child. This undermines your parenting in many ways.
First let's discuss how it undermines your ability to discipline your child. Remember earlier in this book I mentioned that children, even your own, like to test the boundaries of relationships. It is how they learn about the limits of relationships. The testing children do is so they know what to expect from people including their parents.

You can expect that your child will test you. You can also anticipate that he will routinely test your promises and threats: your word. Children need to know you mean what you say. If you demonstrate by your actions that you do not, it will impact your parenting negatively. Your child cannot be sure you mean what you say when you say it. It impacts parenting so greatly because I am not just talking about discipline; I am talking about the relationship between you and your child. If you don't follow-through with your word when you are disciplining, why would you fol-low through with other promises? The child makes sense of this parental behavior this way. "If you say you are going to take away my TV time and you don't, how can I believe that if I tell you the truth (like you told me I could) that I will not get in trouble?" "If you say I cannot go to my friend's house if I don't take care of my mess and then you let me go anyway, why should I be-lieve when you say 'I love you no matter what?" Even though many of the promises you make to your child will feel inconsequential to you, like they don't amount to much, those promises are a big deal to her. Children will generalize, meaning when you are not a person of your word in one situation, they will expect that you will not be in other situations or circumstances.

This next story illustrates nicely the importance of being a person of your word.

**Can you walk away from sushi?**

Some of us moms thought it would be fun to take the kids out for sushi. Alright, I am lying. I should say, some of us moms wanted sushi and had no childcare options so we brought the kids along. Seven of us met for dinner, three moms and five typically well-behaved children. These children had frequented restaurants and knew what was expected of them in terms of their manners.

We got settled in, ordered our drinks and food, and engaged in some conversation. While we waited for our orders to arrive at the table, Jack put his little foot up on the table. Conversation stopped and all eyes were on six-year-old Jack. Jack's mom sternly said, "Jack, take your foot off the table." Jack, who evidently was in a testing mood replied, "Who's going to make me?" The other mom and I had to look away. We knew that whatever came next was not anything we wanted to see; things were about to get ugly. The children, on the other hand, sat and stared, mouths gaping, wondering what would happen next. Jack's mom put her face in Jack's face and whispered through clenched teeth, "If you don't take your foot off the table, we will leave. I'm going to count to three." Way to go Jack's mom! I am about to high-five her for setting a clear limit and consequence, and then something went terribly wrong. Jack did not remove his foot from the table. She counted to three and told him again that she will leave. His foot still remained on the table. She's still sitting at the table and so is he. In my head, I had now counted to seventy-eight, which is well past three, so I was wondering why she hadn't packed up and left. Although I am wondering why they hadn't left; Jack is not. He knew his mom would not pass this test. He knew that she would not be a woman of her word or follow-through on her threat or promise. He knew she would not walk away from sushi. How did he know this? Because in his first six years, Jack's mom had demonstrated many times that her word could not be trusted.

*Breach of promise is a base surrender of truth.*
*Mohandas Gandhi, humanitarian*

Jack took his foot off the table when the food came out because he wanted to—not because he was worried about any consequence. This exchange made me very sad. Sad because Jack did not trust that his mother was a person who meant what she said, and said what she meant. It also made me sad because I knew that this dynamic would play itself out over and over again as Jack grew up. I also knew that the tests would become much more serious and have more detrimental consequences and implications as he moved from childhood to adolescence (I will talk more about that later in this chapter).

On the way to our car after dinner, my four-year-old son who was with us at the restaurant said, "Momma that was not nice of Jack to put his foot on the table."
I agreed, "Those were not good manners. I am glad you know that."
He added, "Also Momma, if that was me with the feet, we really would have left our friends at dinner."
I smiled. "Yes, Andrew, we would have."

You might be wondering how my son knew I would have left dinner? I'll tell you how. I have had opportunities, like all other parents, to prove to my children I am a woman of my word. There have been times when I haven't followed through and my children have called me on it, "But you promised!" When they highlight that I am not sticking to my word, I have to make a choice about how I want to be viewed as a parent (and a person for that matter). I want to be viewed as someone who keeps her promises. That means that if I promised I would take them out for ice cream after dinner and now it's after dinner, and I am so tired I can barely put a sentence together, guess what I am going to do? Yes, you guessed it; I am going to take them for ice cream. My son knows that.

He also realized that, when he was crying in the store and making a scene because he wanted those Pokemon cards, when I said he could get them tomorrow after he did his chores, I would take him back to the store. Did he do his chores without being whiny? You bet; he even did them with enthusiasm.

What about when we were on our way to the mall and I told him and his sister if they did not stop arguing and being cruel to each other, that I would turn the car around and go home even if it was me who wanted to go in the first place? Neither my son nor my daughter believed me that time until you know what happened? I turned the car around and went home. It didn't matter that they changed their tune and promised to knock it off after I stopped and headed back in the other direction. It did not matter that my son gave me that look where his eyes well up with tears that makes it near impossible to discipline him, and it did not matter that I really wanted to go to the mall. What did matter was I stuck to my word even though it was uncomfortable. I followed through because I knew my kids needed to know that I would follow-through.

Trust in the parent-child relationship is compromised when you do not keep your word. I shared why that could be detrimental to your relationship with your young child. What happens as your child enters adolescence if you have not been a person of your word?

*Teenagers are people who act like babies if they're not treated like adults.*
*MAD Magazine*

### What is he going to do, ground me?
Kevin was mandated for counseling services as a consequence of being expelled from school. Fifteen-year-old Kevin had threatened to burn the school down. Prior to the threat, Kevin had been disruptive but never aggressive or violent. Kevin was a charming, bright, young man. He did not feel any remorse for the threat because, as he said, "It was a threat—just words."

I also had regular consultation sessions with Kevin's dad. Kevin's dad was angry and embarrassed. He was a prominent member of the community, and he viewed his son's behavior as a disgrace.

I received an emergency phone call from Kevin's dad. Kevin had taken the car and was driving around town (underage and unlicensed). We first discussed safety issues and then I inquired about consequences legal and parental. Kevin's dad said Kevin would have to deal with the legal consequences if he got caught. "And what about your consequences for him?" I asked.

Pause. Long pause. Dad then said, "I can take away his phone for the weekend."
Now I'm the one who needed the pause because what I wanted to say was, "You have got to be kidding me! That's it?" Instead I said, "That seems fairly lenient."
Kevin's dad said, "You are right. I'll take the phone away for the whole week." I still thought that Dad was letting Kevin off the hook. I didn't challenge him though because I could hear the stress in his voice. I planned on revisiting this in a future parent consultation.

A few days later Kevin comes in for his appointment. I notice he has his phone in his pocket. Hmm. He tells me about his escapade with the car. I say, "I bet your dad was mad."

Kevin's response, "What's he going to do, ground me?" Confused I said, "I would think so, but by the way you are saying it, I guess not."

Kevin replied, "My dad hasn't followed through ever. He's not going to ground me like he says. I can't imagine what it would take for him to stick to what he says. I threatened to burn down the school, and I stole his car! He's too busy being 'Mr. Pillar of the Community' to really parent me." Kevin was able to very clearly state what children and teens feel and think when parents do not keep their word— that we, as parents, do not care.

If you haven't been a person of your word with your child when she was younger, you may be in for more than some typical relationship and parenting challenges with your teenager.

Whether it's a matter of discipline or a promise of a special day, or "I'll be off the phone in two minutes," you must keep your promises to your children. They need to know that you care and they can count on you.

*We must not promise what we ought not,*
*lest we be called on to perform what we cannot.*
*Abraham Lincoln, 16th President of the USA*

## Principle #16

### Never, ever embarrass me.

*Praise your children openly, reprehend them secretly.*
*W. Cecil, writer*

Feeling embarrassed or ashamed is among one of the worst emotional experiences a person will have. When you are embarrassed or shamed by the person or people who are your heroes and caregivers, your parents, the impact of the embarrassment is much worse and has a longer lasting impact.

Take a moment to write down the answers to these questions:
What things did your parents say or do that embarrassed you when you were a child?
_____
_____
_____

How did you deal with it? _____
_____
_____

How does bringing up that memory impact you right now? _____
_____
_____

I can remember overhearing my mother talking on the phone to her friend about the goings-on of the day. Earlier that day I had accidentally slammed the door on my sister's finger. My sister was not injured seriously, but I knew I had hurt her. I felt terrible. Later, when I heard my mom on the phone, retelling the story, I recall feeling so embarrassed and cried to myself in my room while discussing my inner feelings with my cat. I was nine. I'll do the math for you. That was over thirty-five years ago. It wasn't that my mom had told her friend about what happened that was embarrassing. What I felt ashamed about was being careless, so careless I hurt my sister. When my mom retold the story, I felt as if she was making my carelessness public (she wasn't, those were messages I was giving to my little-girl self).

Take another moment to ponder these questions and jot down the answers (I'm asking a lot of you in this chapter, I know):
When was the last time you felt embarrassed: _____
_____
_____

What did you feel embarrassed about? _____
_____
_____

How did those feelings of embarrassment impact your day or any of your relationships (including your relationship to yourself)?_____
_____
_____

Does your recent experience of embarrassment give you any ideas about what it is like for your child when she feels ashamed? _____

_____

_____

Why I ask about your experiences and share mine with you is because it is my hope that you can appreciate what it is like to be embarrassed by your parents and what sorts of things children may get embarrassed about. Certainly, there are going to be times when we embarrass our children simply because we are who we are as parents; those moments are not what I am talking about. I am talking about deliberately embarrassing your child. Embarrassing your child purposely is a sure way to sabotage your relationship with your child. If your relationship with your child is not good, strong, and based in trust, then you can expect that your child will not be cooperative, thoughtful, emotionally healthy or well-behaved.

### Ethan is naughty in school

Ethan loved coming to his play therapy sessions. Like many of the children I see for counseling, he rarely showed me the more troublesome behaviors that he exhibited in school and at home. During counseling sessions, I had first-hand opportunities to observe Ethan lie and steal, use foul language and throw things in anger. At home and school these behaviors made more of an impression because they affected more people and happened in settings that had more stringent rules.

I knew Ethan wasn't an easy child to have at home or in the classroom. His mother wanted to make sure I had a clear understanding of how poor his behavior had been at school. She brought with her and handed me a four-inch stack of reprimand notes Ethan had acquired in his first month of school. She said, "I just want you to see what he is up to in school. It's bad, real bad." As his mother was passing me the stack, Ethan jumped up and grabbed them saying, "Don't look at those, Jodi. Then you won't like me either." He turned to his mother, "I hate you for embarrassing me. I hate you forever."

What an unsettling scene. I worked with both of them during that counseling session to repair some of the damage that had been done in that exchange. In reflecting on what happened, Ethan's mother was able to see that she could have shared those notes privately or had let Ethan know that she was going to give them to me. The bottom line was that strain on their relationship, a relationship that was already very shaky, could have been avoided.

My children provide me with many stories that are worth sharing with my students, workshop participants, and with you too of course! Many of the experiences I had and the lessons I've learned from my children can easily be translated into lessons in parenting. For this book and for other professional and personal endeavors where I want to share these stories about my children, I make it a rule to ask their permission first. I don't want to share a story that would embarrass them. You might be thinking, "How would they even find out?" Well they might not find out, but I would know. I would know that I shared something about them that I had the honor of learning, knowing, or experiencing because I get to be their parent.

**"I will embarrass you in front of all your friends."**

Ethan's mother did not intentionally embarrass him. She did not realize how protective Ethan was of the image that he had demonstrated in counseling and in his relationship with me. Although he was no angel in counseling, he was better behaved than at home and in school. He enjoyed the feeling of being liked by me and equated that to his behaviors in session.

Some parents view embarrassment as a way of disciplining or punishing their child. It gives them a sense of power over their child. Years ago I was one of several parent chaperones on a school field trip with my daughter's class. During the trip a little guy in my daughter's class took his mom's phone out of her purse without asking. His mom was pretty angry. She yanked the phone out of his hand and spanked him on the bottom right in front of the other children and parents, humiliating him. She said, "How do you like that? I will embarrass you in front of all your friends. Don't go into my purse ever again."

It was a difficult scene to watch. There were so many other discipline choices available to Mom. Did embarrassing that eleven-year-old, 5th grader work? Will he ever take anything out of her purse again without asking? Probably not, but what did he learn about what he did and how he did it? What did he learn about his mom, their relationship, and himself?

He learned fear. He learned to fear his mom and the feeling of embarrassment. There may be some positive things that come from this, like he may think twice before he takes something of Mom's without asking. However, most of what he learned is that he cannot trust his mom. If he makes a mistake, it is not okay and beyond that, she might even point it out publicly to hurt him (emotionally). He also learned that people who love and care about him also may turn on him if he upsets them. It's hard to trust someone when you are worried about how they might react.

What do you do if you embarrass your child? Empathize and apologize. Be very clear that you can see they feel embarrassed and ashamed. Tell them how you know this. For example, "I see tears welling up, you must feel embarrassed." Next, apologize "I am sorry I did not know you did not want me to tell Grandma about what happened in school." Your children will forgive you for almost anything. When you sincerely apologize, it means something to them. It also encompasses several other parenting principles. The effect of apologizing, therefore, is compounded resulting in maintenance of a strong and healthy relationship with your child.

*Embarrassment is a villain to be crushed.*
*Robert B. Cialdini, author & professor of psychology*

Principle #17

Tell me "No."

*Parents who are afraid to put their foot down usually have children who step on their toes.*
*Chinese Proverb*

How can I possibly tell my child "no?"
The simple answer to this is because you have to. When your child started toddling around, putting things in his mouth that he could choke on or touching things that could be dangerous, you said, "No." When your little one tried to climb the stairs but was still too wobbly to navigate them safely you said, "No." You said "no" because you were keeping him safe. You will need to say "no" as your child grows for the same reason—to keep him safe. Life will tell all of us "no," so it behooves our children to know what that's like. They will learn frustration, tolerance, how to delay gratification, problem solving, and negotiation skills; all from being told "no."

Saying "no" is part of discipline. Discipline is what helps a child to learn boundaries, safety, problem solving, and responsibility. If you choose not to say "no," you are choosing not to discipline your child. You are also choosing not to teach your child about boundaries, safety, problem solving, and responsibility. I don't think you want that for your child.

It's hard to say "no." There are many so-called reasons for not saying "no" to our children. For example:

- He will cry.
- She will throw a temper tantrum.
- All her friends are allowed.
- It's better to say "yes," then she will sit still.
- He'll just do it anyway behind our backs.
- He deserves things I did not get.
- I don't want to be the mean mom.
- She will hate me.

No matter how many ways we convince ourselves that we should not say "no" to our children, there are many more reasons, better reasons, for making sure we do say "no." We know our children better than anyone else. As parents, we all have expertise—we are the experts of our children. I know when my daughter is lying, when my son is nervous, and when they need time away from others to just chill out. You would not notice these things in my children, but I am sure you notice them in yours.

Being an expert on our children also means we know when to say "no." What happens is we get talked out of it. It goes something like this:
Child: "Can I get this candy?"
Parent: "No, you have a ton of candy at home. We will be home in five minutes."
Child: "Pleeease."
Parent: "I said no."
Child: "But I don't have this kind at home and this is my favorite (whining)."
Parent: "Stop whining."

Child: "I just really want it (still whining)."
Parent: "You know what, fine, I'll buy it. Don't ask for another thing while we are out running errands."

Sound familiar? It does to me. I just had this exchange a week ago (I told you I make mistakes). What is missing from the above example is the how that very stern "no" turned into a "yes." Let me highlight for you what was happening below the surface. It wasn't the child who talked the parent into buying the candy. It was the parent who talked herself out of sticking to her legitimate reason for saying "no." You can get a sense of self-talk in the italics below.

Child: "Can I get this candy?"
Parent: "No, you have a ton of candy at home. We will be home in five minutes."
*There I did it. I said "no," set a limit, and meant it.*
Child: "Pleeease."
Parent: "I said no."
*I hate when he begs. Nice try kid. No means No.*
Child: "But I don't have this kind at home and this is my favorite (whining)."
Parent: "Stop whining."
*I can't stand the whining I would do anything to just make it stop. Oh great, there's Penny from the office, and my son is about to make a scene. She's going to think I am a crappy parent.*
Child: "I just really want it (still whining)."
*Terrific, now Penny is making eye contact. I know she's saying to herself, "I can't believe Jodi specializes in working with children." She probably thinks I am a fraud.*
Parent: "You know what, fine, I'll buy it. Don't ask for another thing while we are out running errands."
Whew. There, now he shut up and I'm no longer being judged by Penny about my parenting skills. I wonder why I am feeling angry and disappointed.

Parents, including myself on occasion, are not confident about their parenting. When you are not confident about how you are parenting your child, you don't trust yourself. In these situations, we make parenting decisions not based on our parenting values and principles, but on what we have convinced ourselves others think would be good parenting. I mean we forgot what is important to our parenting values, values like "No means No" in the above example, for an irrational belief that *if our child is whiny that makes us a bad parent.* These beliefs, that there is a perfect way to parent or that our child's misbehavior is always a reflection of our poor parenting undermine our ability to stick to our parenting principles.

If you say "no candy" to your child and she throws a fit, you may have to leave your things at the register and carry her out of the store kicking and screaming. The idea of that scene may be enough to make you so anxious you already have a stomach ache. The good news is that this only has to happen once. Your child will learn very quickly that when you say "no," you mean it. You will learn you can live through a little embarrassment. Plus, it's very freeing for other people to know what you have known for a while—you're not perfect (see Principles 9 and 15 about making mistakes and meaning what you say).

### Teenage Style Tantrum
Carly was referred for counseling after she attempted suicide. She was treated and released from the emergency room under the condition that she attended an emergency counseling appoint-

ment with me within twenty-four hours of her release.

Carly was a stunning sixteen-year-old. She was dressed impeccably in very fine clothes, and her nails looked professionally manicured. She certainly did not look like a person who had consumed handfuls of pills and had to have her stomach pumped less than twenty-four hours ago.

I asked Carly if she could tell me what led up to her suicide attempt. She shared that her birthday was coming up in the next month, and her parents had promised to buy her a new car. The day of the suicide attempt had been spent at car dealerships. At the end of the day, her parents gave her a choice of cars. She could get a Honda Accord, Nissan Altima, or a Toyota Camry. She said, "I want a Cadillac Escalade. We are very, very rich. My parents can afford to buy me the car I want." This was the reason she tried to kill herself (I did some research; these car choices are in the $30,000 range. The Cadillac costs over $60,000)? A choice of brand new $30,000 cars was a precursor to suicide? Indeed, it was.

I very gently asked this fragile young woman, "Carly, you tried to kill yourself because your parents said 'no' to an Escalade?"
Carly explained through her tears, "But I want an Escalade. They have never told me 'no' before."
If I wasn't sure about the importance of saying "no," before, Carly helped me understand the value in saying "no" to my children regardless of how difficult it can feel.

There are some occasions where we say "no" to our children and there's no good reason. Like when my daughter asks, "Can we listen to 97Q instead of this radio station?"
I say, "No."
Then my daughter asks, "Why?" I have no good reason unless my reason is to prove that I have the power and control, or I do not like the music on that radio station (which wasn't the case in this example). It is important to know why you are saying "no." If you are always saying "no," you lose credibility as a parent because your child does not feel listened to or understood (see Principle 5) and that does not make for a good parent-child relationship.

If you hardly ever say "no," you lose credibility as a parent because your child cannot be sure you will keep them safe. Your child will also have zero experience with being told "no," which will not work out so well for them in life. They will be told "no" and they will have to learn how to manage and problem solve because of it. Without that experience of having to deal with being told "no" in the parent-child relationship, children are left without personal resources for handling the "no's" that they will certainly hear in other settings, like day care, school, and even at the homes of friends and family. Lastly, if you say "no" but don't stick to it you also lose credibility as a parent (see Principle 17). Saying "no" is only half the equation. You have to stick to it. It may be difficult, but it is much less difficult then dealing with a child who does not respect or trust you.

Some of the biggest parenting tests of your parenting principles and values will be around this very principle of saying "no." You can anticipate power struggles. When you say "no" (and stick to it) you are asserting your power in the parent-child relationship while simultaneously letting your child know that you care enough about her to keep her safe.

*Discipline doesn't break a child's spirit half as often as the lack of it breaks a parent's heart.*
*Anonymous*

Principle #18

Let me try.

*Don't handicap your children by making their lives easy.*
*Robert A. Heinlein, science fiction writer & author*

**Can you butter my bagel?**
Lizzy is a super-cute, sensitive little girl. At ten years old, she excels in school academically. She has many friends and enjoys playing sports. She behaves well. Her parents are very caring and love her unconditionally. Her parents also value a super-tidy home. Lizzy's strengths are not associated with being neat, clean, and tidy.

I was lucky enough to be seated next to Lizzy at a breakfast celebration. Lizzy and I know each other well and were having a lovely conversation. Her mother was attending to her younger brother, so Lizzy felt comfortable asking for my help (I see this as an honor as many kids are afraid to ask for help). She asked me to butter her bagel. She already had the bagel on her plate so I passed her the butter and a knife. She stared at me. Had she never seen butter in stick form? Was butter code for some other spread used on bagels? Did I have something hanging from my nose?

Since I was not sure why she was staring at me, I asked, "Lizzy, here's the butter and a knife, what else do you need?"
Lizzy replied, "I don't know how to put the butter on." What? Really? She was observant enough to read my facial expression and added, "My mom always does it." Oh.

I asked Lizzy if she wanted to try, knowing that at ten she certainly had the fine motor skills to butter a bagel. I also trusted that she would not hurt herself or make a mess that would be difficult to take care of. In a very meek voice she said, "I am a little afraid to try."

The story of Lizzy helps us see how important giving your child opportunities to try, is. Trying allows children to learn lessons and experience feelings that are building blocks for good relationships, problem-solving skills and good self-esteem.

**What happens when we let children try?**
What happens when we give children opportunities to try? Whether they succeed or not, they learn and integrate at least eight important life skills. This should you give you a sense of how important this principle is. You'll notice some of these overlap. That's good news because it means these skills build on and are influenced by each other. Therefore, when your child experiences frustration, for example, there are several complex life skills that are being processed.

> Trying allows children to:
> 1. Experience frustration
> 2. Problem solve
> 3. Develop coping skills
> 4. Feel a sense of pride

5.  Gain self-esteem
6.  Learn when they need help
7.  Learn how to ask for help
8.  Set goals

**How can parents assist, what should they be doing when this is happening?**
You may think that it is strange that I include experiencing frustration as something you want your children to go through as a parent. You may even be thinking, "Isn't that cruel to allow them to suffer in frustration?" Let me explain.

When children experience frustration, they learn how to manage the feeling of frustration. Children who do not develop ways to deal with frustration become adolescents and adults who move too quickly from frustration to anger, rage, or helplessness. Because some teens and adults did not have enough experience managing their frustration, they become easily frustrated with themselves and/or others, not knowing how to cope or problem solve.
Lizzy wanted to give up. She was scared to try. How do you imagine that would impact her in other situations where her mother isn't available to solve the problems (small and large) that Lizzy will likely encounter?

What do you do as your child is struggling with a task? You can wait patiently for her to ask for help. You can even say, "I see you getting frustrated. I will be right over here if you want my help, just ask." What you don't do is help without being asked to help. You will most certainly be met with, "No, I want to do it myself!" Think about what it's like when you can't get the jar cap off the sauce. Some helpful person who sees you struggling takes the jar out of your hand and gives it a try. They open the jar. What's that like for you? You feel defeated or at least short-changed out of the opportunity to do it yourself. You may be tempted to show your child how to do it. Again, if your child has not asked you to show him, wait until he asks. He will learn more this way and feel better about himself too.

Two bonuses of letting your child try are that they will develop **coping skills and problem-solving skills**. It will not be necessary to teach them these skills. These skills will come about as they try new things and have to figure out what to do, how to make it work, and how to manage their feelings.

The remaining six benefits of letting your child try are summed up in the following story. I have bold-faced them so they are easy to pick out.

**Kasey vs. the Sock**
Kasey cannot get her socks on. She has tried every day for the past week. At three years old this is a challenge. Boy, does she get frustrated. **She slams her foot down, she throws the socks, she yells that she hates socks and she cries.**

When Kasey's dad offers help, she says, **"No." She wants to do it herself.** It is painful for her dad to watch. She struggles and gets upset. It's not fun to watch your child like that. Then, magic happens: she gets the sock on. **Kasey is delighted.** She smiles. She wiggles her toes, admires her sock-putting-on skills in the mirror. She shows her mom, she wants to call Grandpa and tell him. **She is persistent,** tells the sitter, she tells a random man at the grocery store. **She talks**

**about doing it again tomorrow and teaching her brother** how to put his socks on when he is older like her and a big boy. She feels a sense of pride that only comes from being able to do it by herself. Kasey also will gain self-esteem from this experience. Her parents may praise her for being able to do it, but **it is the action of doing it that makes her feel good about herself and assured enough to try something else new or challenging.**

*"I think I can. I think I can. I think I can. I know I can."*
*Little Engine That Could*

When children are given the opportunity to try and adults or older children do not rush in to help, children learn when they need help. That's an important thing to know about yourself knowing when you do and do not need help. It reinforces your child's self-esteem and overall knowledge of their capabilities. Learning to ask for help develops from experiences with trying as well. Some children are afraid to ask for help. Other children ask for help before trying. Giving children repeated chances to try on their own allows them to figure out not just when they need help but who and how to ask for it.

In the process of trying children, like adults, learn to set goals. They figure out what works and what does not. They learn the steps in achieving the desired outcome. They even discover how much effort they need to exert and how much time a particular task may take. Let your children try so they can learn what they are capable of. They may amaze themselves and you.

*"People don't fail; they just stop trying."*
*Bud Boyd*

Principle #19

Practice empathy.
Show me that you understand how I feel.

*A mother understands what a child does not say.*
*Jewish Proverb*

Rory has autism. He struggles in social situations and frequently gets overwhelmed. When he gets overwhelmed, his behavior deteriorates. On this particular day Rory was out of sorts. He was pacing and muttering to himself in the waiting area of the counseling office. Someone entered the waiting room and the door slammed. Rory got startled and threw himself on the floor. He started screaming and punching himself. His mom laid right down on the waiting room floor next to him and said, "Rory I see you got scared, that noise was loud. It is safe here. Jodi is ready for you." Rory stopped screaming and hurting himself. He sat up and said, "Ok. I'm ready to play with Jodi."

Rory's mom had a good understanding of what Rory was feeling. She was able to understand his perspective. She empathized with him. He did not need to continue to carry on because she communicated to him that she understood.

*If you can learn a simple trick, Scout, you'll get along a lot better with all kinds of folks. You never really understand a person until you consider things from his point of view, until you climb inside of his skin and walk around in it.*
*Atticus Finch in To Kill a Mockingbird*

As parents, we often have empathy for our children. We understand how they see the world and how they are feeling about what they are experiencing. We are doing what Atticus Finch recommended to Scout. Sometimes we even feel what they are feeling. Our ability to empathize with our children is that strong. Being able to understand your child's perspective and the feelings that are associated with that perspective, shows that you can empathize with your child. Having empathy for your child is incredibly important to the parent-child relationship and effective parenting, but it's not enough.

In order to be able to get the most out of this principle you have to be able to communicate that empathic understanding to your child. Rory's mom did that when she said, "Rory I see you got scared. That noise was loud. It is safe here. Jodi is ready for you." She did it and you can do it too.

*The great gift of human beings is that we have the power of empathy, we can all sense a mysterious connection to each other.*
*Meryl Streep, Actor*

Let's start with the basics of empathy, understanding your child's perspective. In order to effectively communicate empathic understanding to your child, you have to be able to read their emotions. There are several ways to do this. The easiest and most accurate way is by looking at your child's face. The key is seeing the feeling and then naming it. Before you attempt to name it, ask yourself:

- What feeling (or feelings) do I see expressed?
- When have I seen this expression on her face before?
- If I make that same expression, what feeling do I feel? (You can even try and imitate that expression in the mirror to see if you recognize it that way.)

Some people struggle with the precise word that describes the feeling. If that is the case, you can use a feelings word list (visit our website to find one www.integrativecounseling.us) to both see if you can find the word that is coming to your mind and to broaden your feeling vocabulary. You don't have to limit yourself to finding a word. There may be a facial expression, gesture, sound effect, or interjection (like "YIKES!" for surprised) that easily capture the feeling, even though a word is never used.

Next, you are going to want to clearly communicate this feeling to your child. A couple of hints:
- Make sure the word is not too big (developmentally for your child, like saying "agitated" to a three-year-old).
- Use as few words as possible to state the feeling (you'll lose your child's attention).
- Speaking of attention, in order to gain it, say your child's name.
- If possible, get on your child's level so you can see his face (don't worry if he's not looking you in the eye, trust me he is listening).

Here are some examples of ways to communicate empathic understanding to your child:
- "Greg, you look angry. Your face is all scrunched up."
- "JoAnna, I can hear that you are sad. You aren't ready to leave Grandma's."
- "You were having so much fun playing, Doug, that you forgot to come in and now you are embarrassed because you wet your pants."
- "[Stomp your feet] Fina, you do not want to share that toy."

Sometimes you will get the feeling wrong. It's not a big deal because you gain credibility with your child for trying. Typically, your child will tell you if you are wrong saying, "I'm not angry!" Sometimes he will correct you saying, "I am not angry! I am tired!" There are many great things that come out of these exchanges.
- Your child learns feeling words. When your child can talk out how she is feeling, she no longer has to act it out.
- Your child learns that you make mistakes (Principle 9) and can take feedback (Principle 13).
- Your child has a sense of self-understanding (she knows how she feels).
- Your child feels listened to.
- Your child knows that you care about her enough to try and understand how she is feeling.

This takes practice in order to do it well. I recommend practicing on your pet. ("Asher, you jumped on me. You must be excited to see me!") You can also practice when watching television, in the line at the store, or wherever! I will warn you though, as you get better and better at this, people will want to talk to you more. When people feel listened to and understood, they want to share what they are feeling and thinking, and they want to be connected to you. They will feel like you understand them better than anyone, like you are even reading their minds.

**I don't even have a crystal ball.**
Jackie was a nine-year-old little girl who was having difficulties at school. She was considered to be "bossy" by the other children. The other children did not like her and did not befriend her.

In our counseling sessions, I used a play therapy approach with Jackie. She easily played for the entire session and even included me in her play. One of the ways I connect with children in counseling and play therapy is to demonstrate I understand their experience as children through using accurate empathic understanding. In Jackie's case this meant that when she bossed me around, I would say things like "You love being in control, Jackie." When Jackie got mad because she could not find the toy cell phone, I said, "Jackie, you are so upset it's not where it should be."

Jackie was very fond of playing "house." She decided to be the mom and told me I was the kid. I said, "This way you can be the boss." She smiled and went about her business running the play household. I commented on her play, "You feel calm when you are in charge. When you are not the boss, it makes you nervous."
She stopped in her tracks, turned and looked right at me and in all seriousness said, "Jodi, you are freaking me out. Please stop reading my mind."

*Most people do not listen with the intent to understand; they listen with the intent to*
*reply. They're either speaking or preparing to speak.*
*Stephen Covey*

I wasn't reading her mind, but I was listening to her. I wasn't just listening to her words, but her actions, tone of voice, pace of speech, mannerisms, facial expressions, and body language. When you listen with that level of intensity you catch on to how a person (child, adolescent, or adult) feels in ways that they were not even aware they were communicating. It is powerful.

You will find that if you can do this at even the most basic level, it will change your relationship with your child for the better (and others as well). There's no better way to connect to your child than by listening with empathy and communicating that empathy to her.

Here's a bonus. Expressing empathic understanding to your child also happens to be the key to calming kids down. You see, when Lyla is in the middle of a full-on tantrum and you calmly say, "Lyla, you are so mad at me because I said, 'No more TV,'" Lyla does not have to act out anymore. She knows you got the message; she's mad at you. It is amazing how this works. I use this all the time with children, not just mine, and not just my clients either. Practice—then do it. You'll be amazed too.

Principle #20

I learn from you who I am.

*Your children will become what you are; so be what you want them to be.*
*David Bly*

Your first social group is your family. Each of us learned who we are and who we are not within our first few years of life in our families. This means that children learn how to behave from their parents and other family members. They also learn how to misbehave from them.

In a parenting book, it may seem like a good idea to discuss how children learn misbehavior from their families. I, however, am going to take a different approach to this topic. In this chapter the focus is going to be on how to support your child's prosocial development through your actions. This chapter will highlight what you can do (and what many of you are already doing) that will create a relationship with your child that minimizes the time and energy spent on misbehavior. The focus is on maximizing the relationship between child and parent clothed in respect and love.

*Even if society dictates that men and women should behave in certain ways,*
*it is fathers and mothers who teach those ways to children not just in the words they say,*
*but in the lives they lead.*
*Augustus Y. Napier*

Let's start off with a couple of questions.
How would you like your child to describe you? List five ways.

| 1. | |
|---|---|
| 2. | |
| 3. | |
| 4. | |
| 5. | |

What are five characteristics that you would like your child to possess?

| 1. | |
|---|---|
| 2. | |
| 3. | |
| 4. | |
| 5. | |

Compare the lists. Are they identical? No. I didn't think so. Mine aren't either. For example, I think my children would describe me as someone who is serious, yet I would hope that my children are laid-back or relaxed. How can I raise children who are more relaxed than serious? I have to change. I have to make an effort to show them ways of being that they can respect and emulate.

Often when we think about parenting we think about how we as parents can make children change. We want their behavior to change or their attitudes to change. If that is what we truly want, if we want change, we have to be that change. Therefore, in our relationships with our children, we have to do the bulk of the changing. That's right, it's up to you. Remember Noah from Principle 6? His lessons for parents are relevant here as well.

## But YOU do that?!

Spencer and her mom were having problems in their relationship. Spencer's mom described her as stubborn and obnoxious. She told me, "Spencer orders me around like she is the parent. She barks orders at me."

After meeting with ten-year-old Spencer and her mom separately, I thought it would be a good idea to see them for a parent-child counseling session. Mom and daughter were both angry on the surface and hurting internally. Their relationship was weak. It seemed all that connected them was arguing.

I observed Spencer and her mom doing a collaborative task so I could focus on how they communicated and solved problems together. I then asked each one of them to share the one thing that most gets in the way of the two of them getting along. Spencer spoke up first. She said, "She doesn't talk to me or ask me things. She just yells."
Spencer's mom quickly replied (actually shouted), "I could say the same about you!"
Spencer responded, "See? You are doing it right now." The back-and-forth continued, when Mom said, "So are you!"

Then, it was my turn. I interrupted these two. "So let me get this straight. Spencer, you don't like when your mom yells at you, but you yell at her?" Spencer nods her head in agreement. "Mom, you have had enough with Spencer shouting at you, but you shout at her."
She says meekly, "Yes."
Spencer then says, "If you don't want me to do it, then you don't do it."

It seems so simple and so intuitive when the lessons of parenting come from children. Spencer's lesson about parenting took all the complexity out of an incredibly complex relationship between this mother and her daughter.

There was a long pause after Spencer spoke. Her mom said, "I promise that I will not yell at you anymore." Spencer moved closer to her mom, hugged her, and whispered in her ear, "I can help you be a better mom and you can help me be a better kid."

Spencer's lesson can help us all be better parents. If we want our children to behave a certain way, we have to show them the way. A subtle way of parenting is to act in ways that are consistent with the ways we want our children to behave.

*Children are natural mimics who act like their parents*
*despite every effort to teach them good manners.*
*Author Unknown*

**What's that in your hair?**
During Breast Cancer Awareness month, I can go to a local hair salon and for $10 get a pink hair extension. A portion of the proceeds goes to National Breast Cancer Foundation (to donate, visit https://www.stayclassy.org/checkout/donation?eid=15489).

Several years ago, my daughter and I decided that we would get the pink hair extensions. This is just one of many acts of charity the members of our family undertake. We, individually and as a family, have participated in races for charity, made donations, and raised awareness through participation in charitable organizations. We never directly taught our son to be charitable, he saw us act that way. He wanted to be that way too, and take action to make that happen. He, in turn, modeled that for his peers, with courage and confidence, and they wanted to do it also!

My son, who was five the first time my daughter and I got the extensions, came with us. He was curious about the extensions and asked a lot of practical questions. "Does it hurt? How long will it stay in? Is it glued to your head? What's the pink hair made out of?" We answered his questions as best we could. Then he asked, "So how come you guys even do it?" My daughter, who was nine, explained to my son in total kid language what breast cancer is. He of course asked, "Can boys get it even though they don't have boobies?"
I told him, "Yes men could get it, although most of the time, women get it."
He questioned further, "Like moms, and sisters, and grandmas, and aunts?" My daughter and I nodded. "Then I want a pink hair thing," he said seriously.

I was very proud and then a moment later nervous. "Andrew, people might make fun of you if you have pink in your hair."
My daughter added, "I bet other kindergarten kids will tease you."
He thought about a minute, "I want to do it. I want to help people. You and Daddy help people in counseling and Leah helps people in Girl Scouts. I want to also." Who could argue with that?

The hair stylist who put the extension in asked Andrew if he knew what it was even for, he told her, "It's to help people with breast cancer. People's moms, and sisters, and grandmas, and aunts."
She told him, "You are the only boy who has ever come in here to get one of these. No kid boys, no grown-up boys, just you."
He said, "My dad would get one but he doesn't have enough hair. I bet there will be more boys next year. All my friends are going to want one." Guess what happened? It was just as he predicted!

What will it take for you to make some changes? Below is an opportunity for you to set some parenting action steps for yourself. Although they are parenting action steps for yourself, they will affect you in all aspects of your life. These steps will not just impact you but your children as well.

The best way to set these action steps is to do it with your child's point of view in mind. Ask yourself, "Who does my child need me to be, so she can be her best?" There are a few steps to goal setting that will help with your action plan. First, decide what it is you believe your child needs from you. Then, create a statement in the present tense of the action step you are prepared to take. Make it as precise as possible. Here are a few examples:

1.      My child needs me to be patient.
I am demonstrating patience to my child each and every day during dinner.
2.      My child needs more of my attention.
I am giving my child my undivided attention for a minimum of fifteen minutes per day.
3.      My child needs me to enjoy life.
I am doing something that makes me smile every day.
4.      My child needs me to show my silly side.
I am letting go by joining in play with my child.
5.      My child needs me to show her affection every day.
I am showing my child affection each and every day by hugging and kissing her at least once a day.

| 1. | |
|----|--|
| 2. | |
| 3. | |
| 4. | |
| 5. | |

Doing what it takes to achieve these goals (practice every opportunity you get) will create a parent-child relationship that is based in love and respect. When that is the basis of your relationship with your child, when you honor the perspectives of children, and follow these parenting principles of love and respect, your child will behave because of it. People who feel loved and respected act out in the world with love and respect.

*My father didn't tell me how to live; he lived, and let me watch him do it.*
*Clarence Budinton Kelland*

## About the Author

Dr. Jodi Ann Mullen, PhD LMHC NCC RPT-S CCPT-Master is a professor at SUNY Oswego in the Counseling & Psychological Services Department where she is the coordinator of the Mental Health Counseling Program and Graduate Certificate Program in Play Therapy. She is the Director of Integrative Counseling Services in Auburn, Cicero, Fulton & Oswego, New York. Dr. Mullen is a credentialed Play Therapist and Play Therapy supervisor, consultant, parent coach, and international speaker. She is the author of several manuscripts on Play Therapy and counseling. Her books include "Counseling Children & Adolescents through Grief and Loss" (co-authored by Dr. Jody Fiorini) (2006), "Play Therapy Basic Training: A Guide to Learning & Living & the Child-Centered Play Therapy Philosophy" (2007), "Supervision can be Playful: Techniques for Child and Play Therapist Supervisors" (co-edited with Athena Drewes) (2008), "Counseling Children: A Core Issues Approach" (2011). "How Play Therapists can Engage Parents & Professionals" co-authored with June Rickli (2011), "Naughty No More: A workbook to help children make good decisions," Co-authored with Andrew, Leah & Michael Mullen, (2013), and also with June Rickli, "Child-Centered Play Therapy Workbook: A Self-Directed Guide for Professionals" (2014). Dr. Mullen was the 2008 recipient of the Key Award for Professional Training & Education through the Association for Play Therapy. She is the proud momma of Leah and Andrew.

CPSIA information can be obtained
at www.ICGtesting.com
Printed in the USA
BVHW05s2103031018
529149BV00010B/399/P

9 780979 628771